# AIR
# AND
# LOVE

Dr Or Rosenboim is an intellectual historian specializing in twentieth-century political ideas. She is Associate Professor of Contemporary History at the University of Bologna. She is a trained pastry chef (Cordon Bleu, Paris), and the founder of The Migrants' Supper Club in London. Her award-winning book *The Emergence of Globalism: Visions of World Order in Britain and the United States, 1939–1950* was published by Princeton University Press in 2017. She has written for various international magazines and websites, and co-authored with Ilana Efrati an art and food book, *Orto: Nature, Inspiration, Food*. She has lived in Tel Aviv, Bologna, Paris, Los Angeles, Cambridge and Umbria, and now divides her time between London and Florence.

# OR ROSENBOIM

# AIR AND LOVE

## A STORY OF FOOD, FAMILY AND BELONGING

PICADOR

First published 2024 by Picador

This paperback edition first published 2025 by Picador
an imprint of Pan Macmillan
The Smithson, 6 Briset Street, London EC1M 5NR
*EU representative:* Macmillan Publishers Ireland Ltd, 1st Floor,
The Liffey Trust Centre, 117–126 Sheriff Street Upper,
Dublin 1, D01 YC43
Associated companies throughout the world
www.panmacmillan.com

ISBN 978-1-5290-9812-9



1 3 5 7 9 8 6 4 2

Map artwork by ML Design.

Typeset by Palimpsest Book Production Ltd, Falkirk, Stirlingshire
Printed and bound by CPI Group (UK) Ltd, Croydon, CR0 4YY

*For Alma and Ron*

# Contents

Jurmala
Riga
Rēzekne
Ludza
(Lutzin)
Kovno
(Kaunas)
Moscow
Gorky
(Nizhny Novgorod)
Trzibinia
Krakow
Dnestra
Dnepra
Don
Bad Reichenhall
Odessa
Danube
Black Sea
Istanbul
Izmir-Smirne
Tigris
Aleppo
Euphra
Mediterranean Sea
Haifa
Haderah
Tel Aviv
Rishon LeZion
Petach Tikva
Jerusalem
Alexandria
Nile
Red Sea

N



Chelyabinsk
Orenburg
Ural
Irgiz
Aral
Sea
Kazaly
Syr Darya
Caspian Sea
Amu Darya
Leninabad
(Khujand)
Tashkent
Kokand
Bukhara
Samarkand
Stalinabad
(Dushanbe)
Kurgan-Tyupe
(Boxtar/Qurgonteppa)
Persian Gulf
Indus
0    100    200    300    400 miles
0        200      400      600 kilometres

# *Dramatis Personae*

## THE ASHEROFFS

Abraham Asheroff (Asher) *married first* Tova, *second* Uzbak Fuzailoff, *third* Rachel Douek

*His children:*
*with Tova,* Zion, Meir, Sarah, Eliahu-Zvi

*with Rachel,* Elazar, Sarina, Rivka

*His step-children with Uzbak:* Four sons and daughters including Yohanan and Batya

Zion Asheroff *married* Batya Fuzailoff

*Their children:* Bechor, Hananya, David, Yaakov, Shlomo-Haim, Elisheva, Zvia, Rachel, Penina

Hananya Asheroff *married* Zoulay Fuzailoff

*Their children:* Daniel, Michael, Yehuda, Tamara, Shulamit, Avner

Shulamit Asheroff *married* Yitzhak Mizrahi

*Their children:* three daughters and a son, including Ilana

Ilana Efrati *married* Shlomo Rosenboim

> *Their daughter*: Or Rosenboim

## THE MIZRAHIS, LATER EFRATIS

Yehezkel Mizrahi *married* Joya Ben-Naim

> *Their children*: Luna, Yitzhak, Shmuel

## THE ADIRIMS

Hirsch Adirim *married* Gena-Rivka Kristal

> *Their children*: nine sons and daughters including Abram

Abram Adirim *married* Esther Simanowitsch

> *Their children*: Selik, Hirsch, Haja, Leib, Scheina, Roha-Taube (Tova), Luba, Sima

Selik Adirim *married* Sara Katz

> *Their children*: Hatzkel and Taube-Mere

Hirsch Adirim *married* Sara Goldschmit

> *Their children*: Schmuel, Brocha, Isak

Haja Adirim *married* Mr Brenaizin

Scheina Adirim *married first* Max, *second* Robert Feinson

*Her children:*

*With Max,* Sima

*With Robert,* Ilana and Bella


Roha-Taube (Tova) Adirim *married* Isaac Rosenboim

*Their children:* A daughter and two sons, including Shlomo

# *Preface*

Eating is the most evocative experience. Memories
are grounded in flavours and scents that bring back the sight of
familiar streets, treasured relatives, shared happiness. For migrants
forced to leave behind their material possessions in search of a new
home, recipes are often the only link to the lost homeland. In my
family, cooking was a way to share a history that often could not
be put into words. When we ate together, each dish invited me to
discover a place, a time, an emotion.

As an only child of two working parents, I used to spend a lot
of time with my grandparents. Every day, when I returned home
from school, my grandmother Tova would wait for me by the
kitchen table with a hot meal: orange-bright carrots tzimmes in
a thick caramel sauce, round kneidlach balls in hot chicken broth,
or cinnamon-scented noodle kugel. 'You cannot live off air and
love alone,' Grandma Tova would say, 'you need food!', and she
would load another serving of carrot and cabbage salad onto my
plate. Once a week, I went to visit my other grandparents.
Grandma Shulamit would cook a herby green rice called oshi-
bakhsh with a squeeze of fresh lemon juice, or golden osh-palao
rice dotted with raisins, almonds and carrots. My grandfather
Yitzhak would offer me a spoonful of 'Turkish salad' of red peppers

and aubergine in hot tomato sauce, directly from the pot, or a slice of rich buttery almond and walnut cake.

In 2017, both Tova and Shulamit died, decades after their husbands. Sitting in my kitchen in London, I opened up the yellowing notebook in which I had collected their recipes, and I started to cook. I stuffed quinces with scented green rice, fried crisp and creamy cheese blintzes and baked airy lemon tortes. I stuffed and rolled tangy vine leaves and cooked thick white bean and tomato soup. This combination of global recipes is not unheard of. In fact, Israeli and Jewish families are often a mix-up of diasporas, each bringing along to the match its own culinary legacy. But every eclectic combination is particular; mine unfolded a history of continuous displacement. As I stood there in my kitchen, missing the long afternoons spent cooking and eating with my grandparents, I became curious about the origins of the dishes I loved to eat. My family's food did not represent the culinary traditions of one place: it was the food of the road. As every generation moved from one place to another, their food was a mixture of inherited and borrowed flavours, techniques and ingredients that reflect the inevitable transnational and transcultural reality of those who have lived 'in between'.

*Air and Love* is a book about displacement, belonging and food. My family's recipes guided my historical investigation of the migration routes of my ancestors, across Central Asia, Northern Europe and the Mediterranean. The stories that I uncovered recounted the lives of people who are rarely remembered, because they left but a few documents to record their existence. Yet, as I continued to explore their past, it became apparent that their individual stories of displacement were part of larger flows of people who sought their futures elsewhere in agitated times. The stories of these families reveal a crack in the history of the modern world.

The heroes of my story are the women and men of three families, Asheroff, Mizrahi-Efrati and Adirim, whose destinies crossed paths in Central Asia and Palestine during the turbulent nineteenth and twentieth centuries. The Asheroffs were merchants who travelled from Samarkand in Central Asia to Palestine, the Mizrahi-Efrati family moved around the eastern Mediterranean, and the Adirim family escaped from Riga, via Central Asia again, to Tel Aviv. Their stories extend through time and space, starting in 1863 with the birth of Zion Asheroff in Samarkand and ending – temporarily – today in the London kitchen of his great-great-granddaughter, me.

My ancestors were not the major players in global events, and their stories were largely left at the margins of history. They were, in their own different ways, ordinary people who lived in extraordinary times. A few of them were important community leaders, like my great-great-grandfather Zion Asheroff. Others, like my great-grandmother Joya Mizrahi, lived a much more private existence. Some, like my grandmother Tova Adirim, showed unusual bravery in a time of great suffering. What unites these unsung heroes are the life-changing histories of displacement that they lived through, which filtered into the food they cooked for their families and into the recipes that became their legacy. Together, their stories tell a different history of the modern world, shaped by familial bonds, personal relations, memories and emotions.

*Air and Love* is a history of the modern world in which migration is the rule rather than the exception. My ancestors travelled to do business, to see the holy city of Jerusalem, to pursue adventures or to start a better life. Moving around was, for them, normal life. Jewish migrants like my ancestors created strong cultural, economic and political bonds that connected the Russian, British, Ottoman and Habsburg empires. After imperial dismemberment, these territories were divided into dozens of new nation-states. Today, people rarely notice the important threads linking Samarkand, Jerusalem and Riga, cities that appear to belong to completely different cultural, geographical and political spheres. These cities were, nonetheless, part of an interconnected trans-imperial world, a world that anticipated many of the cultural and economic aspects of contemporary globalization. The stories of my family's past migrations show the importance of these forgotten connections that forged a world of diversity and plurality, a world where people could feel at home in multiple places.

After the First World War, with the rise of nationalist and xenophobic ideologies, states started to monitor and close their borders. Stricter criteria for citizenship and residence expressed a hostility towards 'foreigners': migrants, refugees and anyone who supposedly belonged 'elsewhere'. Despite these limitations on migration, during the Second World War the ancient amber, silk and spice routes were revived by flows of people escaping violence and persecution. Millions, my family among them, were forced to seek a new home. Then as now, mobility rendered people particularly vulnerable to all sort of harm: bureaucratic cruelty, violent attacks, hunger and disease. In my family, stories of salvation through displacement were intertwined with traumatic memories of grief for lost children or relatives left behind.

After 1945, new international organizations were set up to repatriate or resettle millions of people. New legal treaties and agreements defined the rights of migrants, displaced persons or stateless people, refugees and asylum seekers, as states sought to limit and control cross-border mobility. Mass migration became the phenomenon that defined the modern world.

Writing the history of migrants from their own viewpoint is not easy. I could find barely an echo of the lives of my ancestors in state archives. Only a few letters, memoirs and diaries survived. Without documents, their thoughts and opinions seemed unreachable. While I was eventually able to find some official and personal writings by the men of the family, I was lost when it came to documenting the lives of the women. Lacking the usual archival evidence that launches historical studies, my enquiry took a different path, and I attempted to reconstruct the story of these women and men through the food that they used to cook and eat. My ancestors left a lasting legacy in the form of a collection of flavours, techniques and ingredients: a dense groats soup, a creamy potato salad with home-made pickles, delicate dumplings floating in a rich soup. Their recipes became coordinates on the migration map that guides this book.

For generations, women cooked, whether they enjoyed it or not. They inherited unwritten knowledge, skills and recipes from their mothers and passed them on to their daughters. Some felt emancipated by hiring a cook or eating out or buying prepared food. But making food also gave them an opportunity to establish their own place in an unstable world, a world in which their stories would otherwise be left in the margins. It was their way to find a place in history. The protagonists of my story, Tova, Shulamit, Zoulay, Esther, Joya and Batya-Hannah, live on in the memory of those who knew them, and in the recipes for the food they used to cook.

Tracing the histories of these women turned out to be challenging not only due to the lack of historical sources, but also because a matrilineal family history is necessarily complicated by name changes. In every generation women took their husband's last name: my paternal great-grandmother Esther Simanowitsch became Esther Adirim, and her daughter Tova (who would become my grandmother) changed her last name to Rosenboim. Sometimes, a newlywed couple simply invented a new family name to mark a fresh start, as was the case of my maternal grandparents, Yitzhak and Shulamit, who swapped Mizrahi for Efrati. Others changed their name to please a new ruler, like the Asher family who became Asheroff after the Russian Empire conquered their city, Samarkand. In addition, many of the people I describe here changed their first names too, willingly or not: Batya was renamed Hannah after she recovered from a severe illness, and Tova was born Roha-Taube but was renamed by immigration clerks upon arrival in Israel, just like Joya, who was given the Hebrew name Margalit. The elusive lives of these women sometimes feel like almost intentional attempts to escape historical investigation, but they also reflect the invisibility of women in history and the malleability of existence in displacement.

THERE ARE FOUR TALES IN THIS BOOK, AND EACH TAKES the reader on a journey alongside one branch of my family tree to less-known culinary destinations in some of the most beautiful parts of the earth: golden deserts and ice-blue seas, dark forests and ancient cities. Often, these places are described as seen through the eyes of Western explorers and adventurers. But here I will tell their histories through the eyes of those who lived there, and especially those who lived and left.

The first journey in the book (chapters 1–5) accompanies the

Asheroff family on their route from Samarkand to Jerusalem and Petah Tikva. It starts with the discovery of a memoir by my great-great-grandfather Zion Asher, later Asheroff, who travelled back and forth between Samarkand and Jerusalem from the 1870s until the Bolshevik Revolution in 1917. I then focus on two women, my great-grandmother Zoulay and her mother-in-law Batya-Hannah, whose cooking sought to preserve the traditional flavours of Samarkand even in their new homes in the Middle East.

The second journey (chapters 6–7) is a Mediterranean tale exploring the family history of my grandfather, Yitzhak Efrati, who was always reluctant to talk about his past. His parents, Joya Ben-Naim and Yehezkel Mizrahi, met in Jerusalem, but their families have long been Mediterranean people, travelling between the shores of North Africa and Southern Europe, and embracing the local culinary traditions as their own. As successful cosmo-politan merchants, they moved around the Ottoman Empire with ease, until the First World War transformed their lives. Their food, which Yitzhak lovingly shared with me, was a testimony to the rich and hybrid lives of migrants and travellers before the age of the nation-state.

The third journey (chapters 8–10) begins in Riga, a modern metropolis by the Baltic Sea, and then continues south via Gorky to Leninabad in Tajikistan. On a late June day in 1941, just days before the Nazis invaded Riga, my grandmother Taube (Tova) Adirim persuaded her mother Esther and her sisters to take the last train to Russia. This was the beginning of their dramatic journey to salvation. The fertile lands of Central Asia were not only a promise of food in times of hunger and persecution, but also a fascinating crossroads of cultures and flavours that Tova would never forget.

The fourth journey of the book (chapters 11–12) takes place in different parts of Tel Aviv, where the different branches of my family were united. By 1950, displacement was replaced by stability. In a proletarian neighbourhood in the city's south-east, Tova and her husband Isaac settled down in their new home after almost a decade as refugees. In her kitchen, Tova would recreate the flavours of Riga, while discovering new Mediterranean ingredients. In the northern part of town, Shulamit and Yitzhak wanted to fit into the new Israeli society, turning away from the food of Samarkand and embracing recipes that they considered to be 'local'.

Mobility now seemed to be part of the past, with the present offering a new sense of belonging. The newly arrived immigrants Tova and Isaac never returned to the homes they had left behind, and the Jerusalem-born Shulamit and Yitzhak did not even travel abroad until much later. They simply wanted to raise a family, make a living, have a home of their own and put food on the table. For them, home was the place where they could just get on with their lives.

Like most Israelis in the 1950s and 1960s, my family struggled to connect their own newly acquired stability with the tragic losses suffered by the people who had inhabited that part of the world before 1948. Although this silence about the destiny of Palestinian refugees is frustrating, it was hardly unusual or exceptional – then as now. At the family dinner table or with friends, Arab Palestinians were seldom discussed: there wasn't any explicit hatred towards them, nor any awareness of their forced displacement. Palestinian refugees were largely absent from mainstream Israeli political debates, even though the Israeli landscape abounded with evidence of the local Arab society that was no longer there. The experience of migration in itself does not automatically generate solidarity with other displaced persons. But sometimes, instinctive empathy to common suffering can create a new historical awareness. As my grandmother Tova and I watched on the TV thousands of Syrian refugees escaping the country during the 2011 civil war, she sighed and said, 'They are just as miserable as we were.'

THE PASSAGE OF TIME IS A NECESSARY ELEMENT IN THE making of migrant cuisine. The gap between the country of origin and the destination becomes not only geographical but also temporal. For first-generation migrants, the culinary memory is a return to childhood, to the tastes and aromas of days past. But second-, third- and even fourth-generation migrants who continue cooking these recipes often express a nostalgic desire to return to an ancient era before their lifetime, to a place where they never lived and perhaps have never even visited. For this reason, the food of migrants cannot be 'authentic': it cannot have undisputed origins. Rather, it expresses a sensitivity to the impermanence of things; it sanctifies fragments and changes. It is a way of eating and cooking that assumes that identity and belonging are inherently flexible and open to interpretations.

In migrants' cuisines, meals become multi-sensory bridges between places, the lost home and the new one. The way we eat reflects a creative culinary encounter. The Asheroff family cooked a mixture of different cuisines, concocted during the migration journey between Samarkand and Odessa, and from there to Jerusalem, Petah Tikva and the Shapira neighbourhood in south Tel Aviv. It was not exactly what one might eat in any of those places, but a particular combination of them all.

As much as I sought to reproduce the flavours as I remembered them, I had to accept that the way I cook my family's recipes is inevitably different from the way my grandmothers used to cook; not better or worse, simply different. I understood that the original taste of their dishes had disappeared a long time ago, but I didn't want to look for 'authentic' recipes, the only true way of making a specific dish. Instead I was interested in the variations, in the specific and personal interpretations that appeared along the routes of displacement. Without nostalgia or homesickness, my dinners captured an elusive sense of belonging and preserved some of the generosity, compassion and comfort of our family meals together, even though I am far away. The recipes included in the book are an invitation to discover the life of people on the move, taste their memories, and create new ones.

# Chapter 1
# THE ROAD TRIPS OF ZION ASHEROFF, 1875–1882

IN THE UNOFFICIAL 'WHO'S WHO' OF THE JEWISH community of Samarkand, Zion Asher is reverently described as a devout Jew, a successful merchant and a respectable *haji*, a pilgrim to Jerusalem.[1] Born in 1863 in Samarkand, Zion died in Tel Aviv in 1959. In old age, he wrote a memoir that was kept in the family after his death, but it eventually disappeared. I saw it only once, in an exhibition at the Diaspora Museum in Tel Aviv; a red notebook with yellowing pages full of a mysterious script, similar to Hebrew yet indecipherable. It was written in a Jewish-Tajik dialect, a dying language that only a very few people speak today and which almost no one can read. By chance, I discovered that the handwritten manuscript itself had been taken away from the family by an amateur historian who refused to return it, despite his inability to decipher or understand the complicated text. I gave it up for lost.

Two years ago, I received an email from Zion's only living granddaughter, my great-aunt Edna, who told me that years ago she had translated half of the memoir into Hebrew. 'Perhaps you wanted to read it?' She also had a copy of the untranslated second half and hoped I could find a translator. It took me more than a year to find one, a scholar based in Teheran who could read the text and translate it into English. When the file landed in my inbox, it opened a door to the life of my forgotten – yet most extraordinary – ancestor. The enigmatic title, 'Zion's Sorrows', only added to my curiosity.

Zion's story reflected a world in constant flux. When he was born, Samarkand was still ruled by the Manghud emirs of Bukhara. He lived to see his city conquered by the Russian Empire and invaded by Bolshevik revolutionaries. By the time of his death, Samarkand was part of a new Soviet Republic, Uzbekistan, but by then he had been living for a quarter of a century in the Middle East, where he witnessed the foundation of the State of Israel. For almost a hundred years, Zion lived in the shadow of dramatic transformations over which he had no control. His response to the constant global crises was often a change of scene.

Over the years, Zion made travelling a habit, a second nature that later turned out to be an immigrant's life-saving hunch. His memoir reads like a travel journal, tracing journeys between the cities of the Russian and Ottoman empires, moving back and forth between Samarkand and Jerusalem, embracing displacement as the only way to thrive in an unstable world. There was nothing unusual in getting up one day, packing his belongings and setting off to Istanbul, Kokand, Orenburg or Moscow, thousands of miles away. The urge to discover the world beyond his small native city is, perhaps, what appeals to me most in his story. Anywhere he went, he lived like a local. He learned Hebrew, Persian, Russian and, later, French and Arabic to feel at home in the world. One family rumour – which I want to believe – has it that travelling on his own made him a great cook. Oblivious to modern comforts, he was at ease in a tent by an ice-cold river, or in a train station in Moscow, or in his expansive family house in old Samarkand. I envy his cool-headedness and sense of adventure, which vastly exceeded those of his less ambitious descendants.

Reading his words, I felt that I knew this distant man better than many other relatives that I had actually met. While the photos I have of Zion depict a self-consciously serious heavily bearded patriarch, his writing brings to life an exuberant youth who looked at life with generosity and tenderness. He was the kind of man I would want to meet in a faraway chai-khana, the Central Asian outdoor tea house, a man to share a meal with. Zion rarely described the places he visited or lived in, however. Instead, he wrote an unexpectedly sentimental history of his family's rifts and joys, peppered with reminiscences of food eaten and people encountered on the road. He wrote almost nothing about the sights and buildings of Istanbul, but described in detail the time when his cousin there tried to rob him of a large pile of banknotes and a bag of musk. There are few descriptions of the caravan route from Odessa to Tashkent, but a lengthy account of the food he bought, sold and cooked, dishes that got him a free ride across the desert, or saved his wife's life.

Zion's story starts with a feast: a family gathering in Samarkand to celebrate his birth. The firstborn of Abraham and Tova Asher arrived into the world on a summer day, and the desert heat made any food but fruit unbearable. The old city of Samarkand, once a thriving imperial capital, was reduced in the nineteenth century to a small town surrounded by ancient ruins, orchards and fields watered by the desert oases. The proud father wanted to offer the guests luscious plates of fresh fruit, but all crops in Samarkand that year were rotten: the winter frost had left its mark on the city's legendary peaches and apricots; they had fallen off the trees before they could ripen. The customary celebration was more than a family gathering, it was a symbolic event that would mark the child's destiny: it was no good to start one's life with rotten fruit.

The young father sent envoys across the river and over the mountains to Afghanistan, and they returned carrying five kinds of fruit: white melons and purple plums, juicy peaches with bright orange pulp, blood-red watermelons and succulent black mulberries. The mother's family also sent gifts of rolls of dark, translucent apricot paste, a summer sweet that absorbed the hot sun of the desert and the dense flavours of the fruit. The feast would bless the baby's life with abundance, sweetness and luck.

# APRICOT PASTE

### (*lavashak* in Russian, or 'leather')

Pit and halve 1kg fresh ripe apricots. Crush into a smooth paste (by hand or using a blender). If the apricots are not very sweet, add 3–4 tablespoons of caster sugar. Line a large tin with non-stick baking paper, and spread it with a thin layer of the puree. Leave to dry for 2–3 days (or longer if needed) in the hot summer sun until the centre is no longer sticky. Don't leave the tray outside at night. If the weather is not hot enough, bake the apricot puree in a preheated oven, at 90°C (gas mark ¼) for an hour and a half, or until firm and dry.

ZION GREW UP IN A SMALL HOUSE IN THE JEWISH QUARTER of Samarkand, the Mahalla-i Yahudiyan, a gated labyrinth of unpaved streets, narrow alleys and courtyards tucked between the Registan, the square at the heart of the old city, and the Muslim cemetery of Shah-i Zindah.[2] Today, most of the Jewish residents of Samarkand have long gone, but once, this was a thriving neighbourhood made of generously proportioned houses, kept away from public eyes by high walls. Zion's childhood home was a simple Tajik-style single-storey building that surrounded a courtyard with a fruit orchard, a vine canopy and a well for water. Indoors, there were handmade carpets, colourful silk pillows and beautiful suzani embroideries that the women of the family typically produced at home.

Zion's early years were marked by the tsarist empire's military campaign in Central Asia. According to Russian politicians and the press, the colonization of the region would liberate its inhabitants from Muslim 'despotism' by introducing them to the realm of European civilization. Despite these claims, the war was motivated by diverse and at times contradictory interests of international prestige, economic gain and territorial expansion.[3] The victory was not immediate, and the local population ferociously resisted the Russian imperial army. Yet the resistance was short-lived, and eventually there was little doubt that the tsarist army, led by the future governor of the new Russian province of Turkestan, General von Kaufmann, would capture Samarkand and rule over the region.[4] At first, little seemed to have changed: Samarkand remained formally governed by the emir of Bukhara, who operated under Russian supervision. Yet, slowly, Samarkand was absorbed into the imperial commercial and economic sphere, launching a golden age of prosperity and rights for Jewish merchants like the Ashers.

Although Zion later described the arrival of the Russians as a 'miracle', the occupation exacerbated the tensions between Jews and Muslims in Bukhara and Samarkand. The Jewish community, including Zion's father Abraham, helped the Russians in their war against Muslims, who then accused them of treason and retaliated with violent attacks.[5] After Jewish residents complained that their houses were being sacked and burned down by their Muslim neighbours, the Russian soldiers allowed the Jews to loot Muslim shops, which hardly helped restore peace. The Jewish community welcomed von Kaufmann as their liberator and, to show their gratitude, many Jewish merchants Russianized their family names. Zion's father was now Abraham Asheroff.

The new name reflected Abraham's ambition to be part of Russian society, and especially to do business. He became a successful merchant exploiting the newly forged transport connections between Moscow and Samarkand to buy and sell silk cloth, food and handwoven carpets. He set up shop in the local bazaar, next to the grazing pasture in the shade of the Registan. Today the shops seem to offer mainly souvenirs for tourists. In Zion's day they still hosted a lively market that attracted merchants from near and far, but I would not have been invited to browse their merchandise. There were no women among the shopkeepers, customers or idlers who stood around the stalls of fresh and dried melons, handmade silk fabrics and freshly squeezed purple mulberry juice, and only men sat at the local chai-khana.

As a child, Zion helped his father lead his two horses home from the market. It was a short walk, but in his memoir I read how one evening, when Zion was distracted, one of the horses kicked his head so forcefully that for long weeks his injury would not heal. His father called in experts in modern medicine as well as practitioners of ancient potions, who ordered all sorts of treatments, including spreading on the wound the freshly burned ashes of a silk scarf and the dust of a rare mineral, but nothing seemed to help. Abraham made a vow that should his son recover, the family would travel to Jerusalem to give thanks. Five years later, Zion was back on his feet, and Abraham decided to fulfil his promise. In 1875, Zion was ready to embark on his first of many trips across the Russian Empire to the Holy Land.

The wealthy (and less wealthy) merchants of Samarkand had a habit of visiting Jerusalem every few years, often with their families in tow. For a long time, Europeans saw Samarkand as an incredibly remote destination, an exotic trophy for tenacious explorers. But for the local population, there was nothing strange in an annual trip through Russia via the Black Sea to Jerusalem. A holy pilgrimage can easily provide a respectable excuse, if one is ever needed, for an urge to travel. In the opposite direction, a steady flow of religious teachers continued to arrive from Palestine, hoping to revive the spiritual life of the Samarkand community.[6] The exceptionality of the Central Asian routes was only in the eyes of the (Western) beholder.

There is, nonetheless, little doubt that journeying in nineteenth-century Central Asia was not for the faint-hearted. The railway did not reach Samarkand until General von Kaufmann inaugurated his much-anticipated trans-Caspian line in 1888, which connected the city to the Caspian Sea in the west. Before that, people moved by horse-drawn cart or wagon, by boat or river raft. The journey could last months, leaving travellers prey to disease, road accidents and gangs of murderous thieves. Travellers usually relied on roadside inns for a night's hospitality, but Abraham Asheroff had enough friends and relatives along the road who welcomed his family into their homes, so that they never had to sleep in a stranger's bed.

Zion was about twelve years old when the family left Samarkand, in the late summer of 1875. Years later, in his memoir, he wrote about the trip with the enthusiasm of a child, unflinching in the face of danger and discomfort. I can feel his joy at the rare opportunity to see the world at a time when most of humanity lived in the same village from birth to death. But Zion's mother, Tova, was expecting another baby when they left Samarkand, and I wonder how keen she would have been to travel into unknown lands on a horse-drawn cart. A week after they set off, the family arrived in Tashkent. There, they stopped for the winter, awaiting the birth of Tova's fourth child, Eliahu-Zvi.

A century and a half later, I made the same trip in just three hours on the fast train. Yellow sands and green oases quickly shuffled across my compartment's window, until suburban neighbourhoods appeared alongside the railway. I had to imagine not only the experience of slow travelling along the riverbank, but also the city itself. Tashkent was expanded and rebuilt first by Imperial Russia then by the Soviets, who constructed long residential blocks, highways and underground trains, wide avenues and monumental squares. I had to go into the old city centre, not far from the central market, to see the historical mahallas. The mahalla (Arabic for neighbourhood) is the traditional form of communal living in Central Asia. Today, in the cities of Uzbekistan, it is still possible to see densely populated neighbourhoods of low-rise courtyard houses, freshened by water canals and fruit trees, which might resemble the sights that Zion encountered on his way.[7]

It would be wrong to assume, however, that Zion Asheroff's Tashkent was a desolate desert settlement. After just a decade of

Russian imperial rule, Tashkent had already emerged as the region's major political and cultural centre, a wealthy city with more than a hundred thousand residents. Spies, ambassadors, merchants and adventurers sought their luck along its ancient streets, admiring the beauty of its new gilded churches as well as the ancient blue madrassas that rose in the midst of the small white houses, clay huts and market stalls. Today, artists and architects in Tashkent want to preserve the tradition of the mahalla as the true legacy of Central Asia, against the Soviet-built wide avenues and long rows of anonymous proletarian housing blocks.

The cosmopolitan communal life in Tashkent appealed to Zion, who started to feel at home among the Tajiks, Kirgiz, Persians, Jews and Russians who flocked the city. At school that winter he learned Hebrew, Russian and Persian, and in the afternoons he helped sustain the family by working as a translator at the state tribunal. People from all over Russian Turkestan came to plead their cases, and thirteen-year-old Zion listened to the streams of Persian words and repeated their claims in polite, orderly Russian. He had found his place between the old Central Asian world and the new order created by the Russian imperial rulers.

In the spring, the family was on the road again, sailing on a steamboat to Kazakhstan on their way to Orenburg, where Abraham hoped to make good profits selling woollen fabrics he had bought at the Kaminski factory in Akhmachit. On the long journey along the winding river Syr Darya towards the city of Kazaly, Zion excelled in catching large fish. The Syr Darya used to be the largest river in the region, crossing the lands of the Tajiks, Uzbeks and Kazakhs and flowing through the fields into small shining lakes and muddy marshes. It was a thriving source of life in the desert. Wide and shallow, the river wasn't ideal for sailing (often Zion and his father had to get out of the boat and push) but it was perfect for fishing: carp and catfish, barbel and pike, perch and eastern bream were all common species in the river's waters; you could just reach your hand in and take them.[8]

In the Soviet era, anyone who lived along the Syr Darya ate fish. Indeed, they fished so intensively that many species became extinct, especially after the river's waters were redirected to irrigation canals for the Soviet cotton fields. But in the nineteenth century, Muslims tended to consider fish a food fit only for the poor, who would walk into the shallow ice-cold water in the hope of catching a free lunch. It was true: river fish were cheap, nutritious and plentiful, unlike mutton or chickens, which had to be fed and nurtured for a long time before their meat could be served at the dinner table. But not everyone knew how to cook fish well. Local Jewish communities typically ate their fish fried with a cold watery sauce of parsley and garlic, or, on holidays, stuffed with herbs and garlic and cooked in its own sauce, a sort of Central Asian gefilte fish with an intense aroma.

Today, carp has gained an unjust reputation for having a bland and sometimes muddy flavour, but, in the hands of a talented cook, a fresh, fatty carp can be a delicacy. Out on the river, the ability to cook a river fish to perfection was a precious skill. In his memoir, Zion proudly described how the delicate flavour of his fried carp would gain him the favour of a French doctor and his wife, who hired him as a cook on their trip from Odessa to Tashkent. He recalled how he learned to dust slices of the fish with flour and fry them in their own fat until golden and crisp, but he didn't leave a recipe. Recipes, in their modern form, were simply not part of his approach to cooking, which was based on intuition, skill and practice. I try to emulate Zion's method in my own London kitchen. The hot, crisp carp sizzles in the pan, its scent filling the house with memories of far-flung rivers and streams.

## FRIED RIVER CARP

Take 4 thick slices of fresh river carp and dust them in flour. If the fish is fatty enough, fry it in its own fat in a hot pan for 5 minutes on each side. If the fish seems a bit dry, add some sesame oil to the pan. While the fish is frying, mix in a bowl 3 chopped garlic cloves, a handful of chopped parsley and enough water to create a liquid sauce. To serve, dip the hot golden fish in the sauce and eat with fresh bread.

I ROLL ON MY TONGUE THE NAMES OF THE CITIES AND villages the Asheroff family visited on their way. Kazaly, Iamao Kalay, Irgiz, Gol, Orenburg. Some of these places are still marked on local maps, now separated by national borders that did not exist in Zion's time. Then, there were no borders or checkpoints: just fields extending into the horizon. But the imperial peace was an illusion. In the Batum province on the Black Sea, in today's Georgia, nationalist movements in the Balkans generated a skirmish between the Russian and Ottoman empires. The echoes of the confrontation travelled as far as Orenburg in southern Russia. Lying on the Ural river, between Asia and Europe, the city was an indispensable stop en route to Moscow. As the fighting continued far away, no foreigners were allowed to enter or leave the city.

For months, Zion and his family were stuck in Orenburg because they could not prove they were Russian subjects. The citizenship rights of Samarkandi Jews were far from clear.[9] Technically, they were subjects of the Bukhara Emirate, which gave them some rights of travel, trade and residence in the Russian Empire. They could not enjoy the benefits of full Russian citizenship, unless they proved that their ancestors had lived there for generations. In the absence of official records (many documents in Samarkand's public archives and in people's homes had been burned and destroyed during the Russian invasion), all they could rely on was the personal testimony of the community's elders to support their claim. Getting official recognition of citizenship rights – and of people's very existence – was complicated, expensive and time-consuming.

In Orenburg, the Asheroff family discovered that the papers they had were not the right ones. They had a proof of residence in Samarkand, but no proof that they were citizens. They were no longer legitimate travellers, but foreigners who had to be controlled, checked and approved. This, as they found out, took time. 'A long wait – a heartache', Zion wrote about the family's stay in Orenburg. Against the cold bureaucracy of border control, Zion and his family did not react stoically: they cried and prayed, begging the Russian bureaucrats to turn a blind eye, to acknowledge their good faith. Today, the sight of migrants begging at a closed border is so common that it has become almost normal. The Asheroffs found it a distressing novelty, an omen of changing times.

Eventually, a local trader intervened on Abraham Asheroff's

behalf and convinced the governor to issue the desired travel permits. Even many years later, Zion could not forget the sorrow of being – albeit briefly – an undocumented migrant, almost stateless. Reading about their narrow escape, I couldn't but notice that help came from another immigrant, the trader's family having also arrived in Orenburg from Samarkand. Perhaps he had considered the Asheroff family a little less foreign than others did. It was he who then waved them off as they embarked on the train to the imperial capital, Moscow.

Today, Abraham's chosen route from Tashkent to Odessa seems unnecessarily long and roundabout. For the first leg of the trip – from Tashkent to Orenburg – there were few alternatives at the time. But a quick look at the map reveals the apparent senselessness of going from Orenburg to Odessa via Moscow: travelling east via modern Syzran and Kharkiv seems much quicker, instead of making a long detour up north to the capital. At the time, though, it might have been safer than the more direct route across the Caspian Sea, and could have provided Abraham with business opportunities on the way. He might have hoped to strike a commercial deal in Moscow before leaving the region for a long time. Also, in 1877–8, when the Asheroff family crossed the region, they could hop on the very first railway lines between Orenburg, Syzran and Moscow. Historians rightly see the expanding Russian railways in Central Asia as an imperial tool of conquest and domination; nonetheless, the routes offered local residents some advantages too: a secure and relatively quicker means of transport in and out of the region.[10]

It was Zion's first railway trip, and in his memoir he called the train 'a chariot of fire', a biblical image to convey his amazement at this human-made creation. The trip, with a change of trains, lasted three days and nights. The rattling sounds, astonishing speed and modern comfort of the train left a deep impression that only paled in comparison with the incredible sights of Moscow itself. Zion could not contain his excitement looking at the approaching metropolis from the glass windows of the train. The expansive city, with its many railway stations, crowded streets, modern shops, elegant palaces and fast coaches, was immense and terrifying, full of adventures, opportunities and dangers.

When the family had settled in their temporary accommodation in a small flat above a shop, they welcomed a group of visitors from Moscow's Jewish Bukharan diaspora. Only then did Abraham notice that their bag of bread was missing. To the modern traveller, it would seem absurd to travel across the Russian Empire with an 80-kilo sack of bread, and even more ridiculous to lose it. But the familiar noni-tokhi, which is a thin crisp cracker made of flour, water and salt and sprinkled with caraway seeds, could have been a homely comfort on the long trip, especially for those like the Asher family who observed the kashrut dietary laws and would not buy bread in local bakeries. Despite the apparent fragility of the friable cracker, noni-tokhi was the perfect travel food: shaped like a bowl, it could easily contain other preparations, and if kept dry, it would remain fresh for weeks. Not unconnectedly it resembles the mythical matzo that the people of Israel baked to eat on their exodus from Egypt.

Women would prepare noni-tokhi at home, seated on the floor, kneading the dough in a large bowl. They then divided it into balls and rolled each into a flat circle on drum-like plates, placed each circle on a round metal plate and baked it in the hot taboon until crispy. More than just food, the bread bag gave a sense of safety in unfamiliar lands.

Abraham suspected he had left the sack on the train when they hurried off at the busy station. Its loss must have been distressing, but not enough to persuade Abraham to change his plans to spend the evening with his Muscovite friends. And so, the task of retrieving the family's bread fell to his eldest son. Zion hopped on a carriage and asked the driver to take him to the train station. 'Which one?' was the unexpected answer. After some negotiations in Russian, Zion managed to arrive at the railway lost-and-found hall, where bags of all kinds were stacked on shelves that covered the walls from floor to ceiling. It was daunting, but he knew he could not return empty-handed. Finding the bag, hidden among unclaimed cases and sacks, was a transformative rite of passage. Zion had proudly entered adulthood.

## NONI-TOKHI

Sift 400g flour and mix with 1½ teaspoons (8g) of salt, ½ teaspoon (3g) of sugar and 1 teaspoons (5g) of baking powder. Pour in 3 tablespoons (30ml) of vegetable oil and gradually add 1 cup (250ml) of water to form an elastic dough (you may not need all the water, the dough should not be sticky). Knead the dough for 10 minutes and leave to rest for 1 hour. Preheat the oven to 240°C (gas mark 8). To give the bread its typical dome shape, grease well the outside of a 30cm wok or a metal bowl with some oil and place it upside down on a baking sheet. Divide the dough into 8 balls, and then roll each ball into a thin circle and sprinkle with caraway seeds. Place a dough circle on the bowl and use a fork to prick holes all over them. Bake for 10–12 minutes or until golden and crispy. Let the noni-tokhi cool down before removing it from the bowl. Bake one circle at a time until all the dough is used. The noni-tokhi can be used as a bread bowl to serve salads or rice dishes, or eaten separately.

THE REST OF THE TRIP WENT SMOOTHLY, BY THE STANDARDS of the era. A brand-new train took the family from Moscow to the port city of Odessa, nestled on the shores of the Black Sea. They did not linger there long and soon embarked upon a thirty-six-hour journey by boat to Istanbul. From Istanbul they took a Russian sailing boat to Jaffa. The boat did not have cabins (or the family could not afford one), and for six days and nights they all sat on top of their luggage on the deck, eating fresh vegetables and noni-tokhi and gazing at the blue horizon of the Mediterranean Sea, which Zion was seeing for the first time. Their journey was coming to an end.

As the harbour came into sight, a storm broke and the captain announced that they would have to continue south to Port Said and return to Jaffa when the sea was calmer. However, if any passenger wanted to disembark now, they could do so via a couple of fishing boats that would risk the rough seas to come out to the boat. Zion's father insisted that no storm would deter him from fulfilling his vow to visit Jerusalem. And so, father, mother, children and luggage were shuffled into paddle boats that fought the waves for two hours before finally reaching the shore. Zion felt 'like a corpse' but they had survived.

In 1878, Palestine was a marginal province of the Ottoman Empire.[11] Not yet the destination of mass Jewish immigration, it was home to many different religious and ethnic communities: Greeks, Russians, Jews, Christians, Turks, Armenians and Ethiopians. Jerusalem was a village that hoped to be a cosmopolitan city, encapsulating all sorts of cultures, habits, flavours and scents in a small walled space, which opened up to rolling hills and expansive pastures. As a relatively small provincial place, Jerusalem felt much more familiar to the Asher family than the imperial capital of Moscow or the sprawling seaside metropolis of Istanbul. Having lived all their lives in a small Jewish quarter next to Muslim neighbours, their ears were accustomed to a mixture of languages and habits. It was easy to replace the sounds of the muezzin calling from the blue-tiled minarets of Samarkand with the muezzin of the domed Jerusalem mosques.

Zion might have felt he belonged in Jerusalem, but his memoir was that of a young man who spent more time on the road than anywhere else. He was at ease on mule-drawn carts along dusty country roads or on steamboats crossing the Bosporus strait, and whenever he returned to his family he felt an itch to get away again. His nomadism, however, was not just a whim; I soon discovered that he had his reasons to leave.

Zion was only fifteen when his father arranged his marriage to Batya, the daughter of Uzbak Fuzailoff, a widow who had also arrived in Jerusalem from Samarkand. Zion's memoir leaves me in the dark about Batya. I want to know more about her looks, her character and her aspirations. I wonder if Zion even liked her, but all that he wrote was her age: Batya was thirteen, too young to marry. Zion refused the match. He stopped studying and idled all day around the market. After a while, though, he realized that 'there was no way out', as he wrote. He dared not disobey his father.

Later that year, Zion and Batya were married. The family rented a room for the young couple in Nahalat Shiva, a newly built Jewish neighbourhood outside the city walls. Their wedding was a luxurious feast, where the guests danced all night, eating eight kinds of fruit that Abraham imported from Samarkand. Yet a few days later, Zion developed a persistent fever. In his memoir, he wrote that the 'public' – by which he probably meant the community's elders – proposed that he should leave town and go elsewhere. Maybe displacement would bring him good health. His father agreed, but instead of sending him to a mountain sanatorium or a seaside resort, as was usual among the European bourgeoisie at the time, he shipped Zion to Istanbul, to launch his career as an international merchant. In her husband's absence, Batya was moved back to Abraham's house, where she was expected to help with domestic chores. After a few months in Istanbul, Zion's health recovered. He started to import silk scarfs from Kokand in Central Asia and to sell them for great profit in the Istanbul bazaar, where he made a name for himself as a confident, sharp and cultured man. But between his words I continue to sense a resentment against a father who insisted on keeping him away, for reasons that would only later come to light.

When the time came to return home, in the spring of 1882, Zion started packing his trunk. He bought special ingredients that could not be found in Jerusalem: red wine from Smyrna (today's Izmir), strong-flavoured Italian caciocavallo cheese, tins of salted bonito and mackerel – which would have been particularly desirable in the mountainous landlocked city. Decades later, Zion described these delicacies in detail in his memoir: the smooth, dense wheels of cheese, the dark red of the wine, the strong-smelling fish covered with silvery salt. He lingered on the food more than on landscapes or monuments; he was enamoured with the flavours and scents of the markets he visited, which accompanied him long after he stopped travelling.

When Zion returned to Jerusalem, he discovered that his father had taken a second wife, against the wishes of his mother, Tova. In an unexpected turn of events, the chosen bride was Uzbak, the mother of Zion's young wife Batya. Taking a second wife was one of the customs that the Samarkandi Jews borrowed from their Muslim neighbours in Central Asia, but in Jewish Jerusalem polygamy was discouraged. Zion recounts that the rabbinic tribunals in Jerusalem only reluctantly agreed that Sephardi Jews could legally marry more than one wife, and they tried to persuade Abraham to change his mind.

No one but the bride and groom seemed happy about this union. Uzbak's sons were unwilling to submit to the commands of a new stepfather. Zion saw Abraham's decision as an act of pure egotism, a pursuit of personal pleasure at the expense of Tova, his first wife. He suffered for his mother, who was against the wedding, but had no power to stop it. The marriage of Abraham and Uzbak explains to me the somewhat mysterious title of the memoir, 'Zion's Sorrows'. He lived his life under his father's command and rarely found the force to resist or challenge his will. The polygamous marriage and the choice of bride were both contested and controversial, even at the time. The extended family and the community's dignitaries opposed Abraham's decision but, as Zion wrote perhaps cynically in his memoir, 'no one could stop a couple in love'. The family rift following the wedding left Zion little choice but to take to the road again, hoping that a change of scenery would bring him the happiness that he lacked at home. Leaving Batya behind with her mother and his father, he packed his few silk coats and linen shirts, his shiny black leather boots and thick wool blankets. He bought a one-way ticket for a Russian boat from Jaffa to Istanbul.

## Chapter 2

# BATYA-HANNAH ASHEROFF IN JERUSALEM AND SAMARKAND, 1887–1914

IN 1878, WHEN THE ASHEROFF FAMILY FIRST ARRIVED FROM Samarkand, they rented rooms in Jerusalem, where most of the other immigrants from Samarkand and Bukhara lived. Yet for people who spent so much time on the road, a stable home promised a new form of security, perhaps even a sense of belonging. Abraham Asheroff, Zion's father, aspired to build a house of his own in his new homeland. In the years that followed, Jerusalem changed rapidly: thousands of European, Yemeni and Iraqi Jewish immigrants brought new energy to the city. There was a sense of innovation, a collective aspiration to transform the millennial holy city into a modern metropolis. But there was no agreement as to how this ambitious plan should be realized. Among the community of Bukharan merchants in Jerusalem there was talk of building new houses on the hills outside the city; in 1894, Abraham joined a group of merchants from Samarkand and Bukhara who bought a piece of land on a hill surrounded by fertile fields, a short ride from the Western Wall. There, he would build a house for his family.

The Asheroff house in Jerusalem would become an important place for the family: many hopes and sacrifices were poured into its foundations. If I could visit the place that became my ancestors' home in Palestine, would I get closer to their stories? Unlike the family's Samarkandi home that has disappeared into oblivion, the Jerusalem one still stands, offering a precious glimpse into their past. On a warm winter day in 2015, I drove to Jerusalem with my grandmother Shulamit. I parked the car in one of the small streets of the old Bukharan Quarter, a quiet neighbourhood not far from the city centre, and we set off to look for the house. Shulamit could not remember the exact location but she was sure that the house stood close to the market. Women and children dressed in religious clothing hurried past us towards a covered street of small household shops, challah bakeries, cheap fishmongers and vegetable stalls. Outside, two old men stood by a small table, selling bunches of scented coriander, parsley, mint and myrtle. The market seemed still to be the liveliest place in the neighbourhood. We made our way between the shoppers and stalls, turned into a side street and reached a metal gate decorated with a star of David. This was the house, Shulamit said.

We pushed the gate open and sneaked in. The house seemed run down, but my grandmother was certain that we were in the right place. She was born here, where four generations of her family had lived, cooked and feasted. The old lemon tree that she remembered was still in the courtyard, bearing dozens of fragrant fruits that filled the air with their refreshing scent.

I have yet to find photographs of the Asheroff house in its prime, but Zion described it in his memoirs. It is a simple square building, made of Jerusalem stone, with a roof of red tiles. Its rooms are interconnected, giving on to a central courtyard with lemon and bergamot trees. There is a touch of the 'Orient' in the four arches supported by stone pillars and in the large terrace with a pyramid-patterned ceiling. It is not the most impressive house in the neighbourhood. I've read that the palatial home of the Yegudaioff family around the corner had fresh water, luxurious Turkish baths, colourful frescos and modern oil lamps, as well as large arched windows to the street, in the 'European' style. The existence of such splendour seems hard to believe, given the building's current state of general desolation.[1] Nonetheless, it is true that in its heyday this poor and decrepit neighbourhood used to be graceful and impressive, with wide tree-lined streets, elegant buildings and modern amenities. In the early twentieth century the Bukharan Quarter was a symbol of modernity, a real-world utopia.

In a dusty second-hand bookshop in downtown Tel Aviv, I found the constitution of the Rehovot Habukharim, or the Bukharan Streets, the neighbourhood now known as the Bukharan Quarter.[2] The public spirit of its wealthy founders is impressive: they required luxurious standards of construction but also allocated generous public spaces. They discussed at length the need for solidarity among the community. They set up a fund to build a poorhouse, public baths and an orphanage, and pledged to adorn the streets with trees and flowers for everyone to enjoy. Rich and poor would all pray together in the same synagogues, their children would attend the same nursery and school, their families would celebrate holiday processions together in the communal gardens. These migrants didn't seek to integrate in the local ways of living in Jerusalem but sought to be free from the shackles of the past that overshadowed the historical centre.

While his father was planning the new family home in this

idealistic, modern neighbourhood, Zion seemed mostly interested in working hard enough to afford a home for himself and his young wife, Batya. He wanted to break free from his father and also to liberate Batya from the chores expected of her at the Asheroff house, but in Samarkandi Jewish families such as his, family ties were almost impossible to sever. As the firstborn son, Zion was expected to obey his father's orders and to take over his role as the family's breadwinner. Abraham sent Zion on frequent trips to Istanbul, Izmir, Samarkand, Kokand and Moscow, to buy and sell goods in local bazaars, and bring to Jerusalem his profits, which were used to pay for the construction of the Asheroff house in the Bukharan Quarter. Zion did not enjoy this arrangement, which kept him away from Jerusalem, and from his wife. For long periods of time, Batya had to live under Abraham's roof and obey his commands.

During one of his visits to Samarkand, Zion met a carpet merchant who invited him to be his assistant. He stayed in the town for four years, enjoying the company of a group of young Jewish textile merchants like himself, who introduced him to the art of trade. At their dinner parties he tasted delicious food and learned about the latest ideas in politics and culture. During this period, he continued to send his profits to his father and begged him to allow Batya to join him in Samarkand. Abraham, however, did not give Zion's letters to Batya, refused to let her leave Jerusalem, and replied to his son that, should he feel lonely, he could simply marry a second wife in Samarkand.

The only way Zion could reunite with Batya was, he concluded, to return to Jerusalem. He had little money of his own, and no job awaited him. He started working for Osman Maha, an Arab fruit merchant who set up business every day by the Jaffa Gate, where merchants put up their stalls of fruit, fresh herbs, bread, lemonade and cakes. It was one of the busiest spots in the city, and Zion, who had a way with words, instinctively knew how to appeal to the crowds. Fluent in Hebrew, Arabic, Persian, French, Russian and Ladino, he could speak with almost any customer in their own language. His gentle, mild manners made him the perfect salesman. At Osman's stall, he sold apples, oranges, lemons and quinces, chestnuts, cucumbers and pears – from sunrise to sunset, until he was able to afford the rent for his new family home with Batya.

The couple's rental flat was small – maybe it was even a room in another family's home – but moving out of the Asheroff house was a big statement in a culture where multiple generations of one family typically lived together. Zion did not seem to resent the idea of sharing a house with his extended family: his act of rebellion seemed directly targeted at his father. When his mother obtained her divorce from Abraham, she moved in with Zion and Batya, keeping the young woman company in the kitchen.

In her new home, Batya began to prepare simple meals that brought Samarkand and Jerusalem together. She roasted whole aubergines on the fire to make boijon. Rather than crushing the aubergine with metal instruments that would have lent bitterness to the smoky pulp, she used a special brush made of turkey feathers that preserved the aubergines' natural sweetness. She seasoned the mashed pulp with salt and chopped garlic, as typical in the Middle East as in Central Asia. But here, in Jerusalem, she also poured on top a swirl of olive oil.

Olive oil must have been Batya's most delightful discovery in her adoptive city. Olives do not normally grow in Central Asia, so their oil was completely absent from Samarkandi cuisine. But olive trees silvered the mountains that surrounded Batya's home. Traditional recipes based on lamb tail fat, cottonseed or sesame oil were transformed in Jerusalem by the fresh fragrance of the local oil which permeated Batya's cooking, eventually becoming an integral part of it.

# BOIJON

Prick a large aubergine with a sharp knife and roast it on an open fire, or in a grill oven, until the skin is crisp and the flesh feels soft to the touch. Let it cool, then carefully slit open the skin and scoop out the pulp. Do not use metal utensils as they blacken the aubergine. Chop some garlic cloves and add to the aubergine. Season with extra virgin olive oil and sea salt and serve with some noni-tokhi (page 25) and a tomato and garlic salad.

Apart from their enthusiastic embrace of olive oil, the Asheroff family didn't fully immerse themselves in the local culture. They continued to wear colourful silk robes that distinguished them from the rest of the population like parrots in a band of ravens. They cooked recipes that they had brought with them from the remote Silk Road, adding dried fruit to meat dishes, and mounds of chopped coriander to their fragrant rice. They slow-cooked their Sabbath lunch in cotton bags and baked their crisp noni-tokhi breads on thin metal plates.

They seemed to indulge in their difference, and sometimes it proved useful. When Zion wanted to return to Samarkand and to take Batya with him, he visited the Russian consulate in Jerusalem to add her name to his passport. There he discovered that a wife was already registered in his passport, and that she was supposedly awaiting him in Samarkand. Suspecting that his father had pulled some trick to prevent Batya from leaving, Zion came up with a plan. Since polygamy was a common practice in Samarkand, he presented Batya to the Russian consul as his second wife. Thus, in 1887, with a valid passport and a bag of fresh vegetables and eggs to eat on the way, Zion and Batya left Jerusalem for Samarkand.

The family now lived parallel lives. In the Bukharan Quarter of Jerusalem, the construction of the new Asheroff house proceeded slowly. It was an expensive enterprise that took the better part of a decade. In Samarkand, Zion's textile trade did well and he built a house in the old Jewish quarter, the Mahalla-i Yahudiyan. The Asheroffs in Jerusalem and in Samarkand were connected by a constant flow of goods, capital and letters that kept the two branches of the family informed of births and deaths, quarrels and investments. There were plans for a future reunion, and Zion bought a piece of land in Jerusalem. Still, the freedom of living away from the oppressive authority of his father was, for Zion, precious.

It was only in 1904, more than fifteen years after they had left, that Zion and Batya returned to Jerusalem. Now in their mid-thirties, they were parents of four children, who lived comfortably thanks to Zion's commercial success. As well as the house in the Mahalla, they built another one in the new Russian part of Samarkand. Zion became known in the city not only as a shrewd businessman, but also as a cultural connoisseur. Not many others in town could read and write in French, the lingua franca of European communications at the time, and he happily volunteered to write telegrams and letters for anyone who asked.

For Batya, though, the years of Zion's ascent to prominence were accompanied by hardship and heartbreak. She had nine children, but lost her firstborn child, as well as three more baby boys before they turned two years old. After the birth of her ninth child – this time, a girl – she fell gravely ill. Zion wrote in his memoir that he did everything in his power to save her. He appealed to modern science and ancient traditions, willing to try even the most improbable remedies. He followed the neighbours' advice to feed her ground fried chickpeas and the juices of roasted meat shishlik or fresh challah. He obeyed the rabbi's order to donate 131 fresh egg yolks to the Jewish community to save her soul. I wonder about the mystical meaning of that number, but the memoir gives no further explanation. Expensive nurses and doctors tended to her for a whole month but offered no relief.

As usual, Zion's tale of his wife's ordeal is mostly a story praising his own inventiveness. Is it absurd to believe his claim that what eventually saved Batya was his cooking? At the doctor's order, he served her chicken soup, which he made himself using a cock slaughtered on the Shabbat. He cooked the meat slowly, with just a few herbs, gently skimming the excess fat off the broth as it cooled. The clear aromatic liquid was pure and nutritious, a golden medicine to restore body and soul.

# CHICKEN SOUP

Take a whole chicken, wash it thoroughly and put it in a large pot. Fill the pot with cold water and bring to the boil. Remove the chicken, throw away the cooking water and clean the pot. Return the chicken to the clean pot, add cold water, a large bunch (about 100g) of mixed herbs (parsley, coriander, dill, fennel, celery), 4 garlic cloves, 1 teaspoon of whole black peppercorns, 1 small onion cut in half, and 2 teaspoons of salt. Bring back to the boil and simmer for 30 minutes. Remove the chicken, and continue to cook the broth on a low heat for another 30 minutes. Pass the broth through a fine sieve and serve it piping hot.

Slowly, Batya regained her strength. Zion washed her hair with almond oil and brushed it smooth. Henceforth he would call her Hannah, meaning 'divine grace', after the righteous mother of the prophet Samuel. He vowed, like his father before him, to take the family on a pilgrimage to Jerusalem, to give thanks for her recovery. Religious devotion might have motivated Zion's decision to travel, but his memoir also highlights his nostalgia for a beloved place he hadn't seen for too long.

After selling all their belongings and closing up their empty houses, Zion and his family set off towards the Mediterranean. For the first time, they were able to travel by train from Samarkand on a new railway line from Tashkent to Orenburg, which was completed in 1905–6. Even though the Asheroffs were able to ride the train only for some and not all of their journey, it made the trip shorter and safer than ever before.

More than a century later, I sat in an air-conditioned, modern fast train from Samarkand to Tashkent on my own way home to Tel Aviv. The passenger next to me took out of her large bag a homely porcelain plate, covered with a tea towel, which she removed to reveal a hearty rice dish dotted with carrots and cumin seeds, with a side of puffy naan bread covered with nigella seeds. She filled her teapot from a hot-water samovar at the end of our carriage and poured black tea into a small blue piola cup. Her lunch certainly seemed better than the usual sandwich sold on European trains and it made me wonder what the Asheroffs ate on their long journey. Did they also pack plates of home-cooked food for their trip to Jerusalem? I can imagine bags of baked dumplings, warm bread and pots of palao, little balls of orange carrot halva and sugared almonds to munch on as they crossed the Russian Empire and the Black Sea.

## CARROT HALVA

Peel and finely grate 5 large carrots (about 400g). In a saucepan, put 400g of sugar and cook it over a low heat until the sugar is melted and very lightly golden. Add the carrots and mix quickly. Cook for a couple of minutes, but don't let the carrots darken. Place the pan in a bowl of iced water to cool. When the mixture is lukewarm, use your fingers to form the mixture into small balls, and roll them in ground almonds. Keep the halva balls in a cool place.

WHEN BATYA-HANNAH AND ZION HAD LEFT JERUSALEM in 1887, the Bukharan Quarter was no more than a dream, but in 1904 they returned to find the neighbourhood in its full glory. An elegant grid of wide, tree-lined streets distinguished it from any other neighbourhood in Jerusalem, and perhaps in all of Palestine. Women in long linen and silk gowns and men in ivory suits promenaded on the pavements. The streets were carefully maintained at public expense. The houses were larger than usual, and their proud owners hosted lavish feasts that became the talk of the town. Their guests came not only from the neighbourhood itself, but also from the Ottoman elite and the old Jewish families in the city centre. The neighbourhood's council felt the need to intervene, to remind the wealthy residents that excessive spending should be avoided when poorer families had hardly enough to eat. But the habit was hard to eradicate; less affluent families also cooked and served meals that seemed exaggerated, luxurious and extraordinary.[3]

The Samarkandi architecture that inspired the Asheroff house in Jerusalem presumed – and demanded – that the extended family would spend time together. The house stood in the far end of the market street, facing the open fields and separated by a high wall from the street. Its courtyard had a garden scented by lemons and bergamots, roses and sweet mint that the Arabs called *nana*. Grandmothers, mothers, aunts and daughters would all sit together in the perfumed garden, cooking, chatting, singing.

Like all other Bukharan houses, the Asheroff house was made for feasts. Every holiday, wedding or even a funeral was an opportunity to eat together. It wasn't unusual to have thirty guests for dinner, all reclining on cushions around a low table, while musicians played the doira drum or the santur. A succession of delicious dishes would be brought in, from whole roast lambs stuffed with rice and herbs, to platters of stuffed pigeons, echoing the extravagance of princely courts. Brightly coloured sweets of all kinds – carrot halva and stuffed dates, fruit preserves, marzipan and sugared nuts – were presented to the diners on large silver plates, alongside an abundance of colourful fresh fruit that was not a common sight in Ottoman Jerusalem. Fresh bread arrived from the large communal Turkish oven, a sort of tandoor that filled the streets with the warm scent of baking.

Echoes of such opulent Samarkandi feasts survived in the family, but what had once been an everyday event became by the 1950s a once-a-year effort. Only on very special occasions did doushpera (meat dumplings) float in my grandmother's blue bowls of red soup of beetroot, tomatoes, chickpeas and carrots, and the guests were limited to close family members only. Doushpera and other dumplings are common enough on Samarkandi cuisine, but my grandmother's red soup entered the repertoire as the Russian Empire brought tomatoes and beets to Central Asia, and they soon became an integral part of local meals. The Asheroffs took the recipe with them to Jerusalem, where beets and tomatoes now grew in their small vegetable garden.

# DOUSHPERA SOUP

Overnight, soak 1 cup (150g) of dried chickpeas in water with 1 teaspoon of baking soda. The next day, rinse the chickpeas and boil them in fresh water until tender. Drain the chickpeas, remove their skins, and put them aside. Grate 8 large ripe tomatoes into a pulp and strain to remove the seeds and skins. Add the tomato pulp and chickpeas to a large saucepan, bring to a boil and remove from the heat. In another large saucepan, heat 2 tablespoons of oil and 1 finely chopped onion until golden. Remove the onions and add to the tomatoes pot. Reuse the same pan to sauté 2 peeled and diced beetroots, 3 peeled and chopped carrots, and 1 chopped celery stick, until golden. Remove the vegetables from the pan and add them to the tomato pot. For a meat version, cut 500g of veal into 3cm cubes and cook on all sides in the sauté pan, then stir them into the tomatoes pot. Add a bunch of coriander and parsley stalks tied with a string. Make sure that the liquids cover the vegetables (add stock or water if needed), season with salt and pepper and simmer over a low heat for 30 minutes.

Meantime, make the doushpera (meat dumplings). Make the dough by mixing 4 cups (500g) of flour, 1 lightly beaten egg, ½ teaspoon of salt and ¾ cup (175ml) of water (add the water gradually – to make a firm dough, you may not need it all). Knead the dough well, cover it, and let it rest for an hour on the kitchen-top. While it's resting, make the filling by frying 1 finely chopped onion in a little olive oil until golden. Remove it from the pan and let it cool. Now mix the onion with 300g minced beef or lamb and 3 tablespoons of chopped coriander. When the dough has rested, roll it into a 1mm-thin sheet, and cut out circles about 5cm in diameter. Put a tablespoon of the filling on each circle and close it into a half-moon shape, then bring the tips together to create a round dumpling. Cook the dumplings in salted boiling water for a couple of minutes. Serve them in the hot soup with a sprinkle of freshly chopped coriander on top.

IN THE EARLY TWENTIETH CENTURY, OTHER MEMBERS OF Jerusalem's Jewish community, however, increasingly frowned upon such frivolity, describing the abundant culinary utopia of the Bukharan Quarter with distaste.[4] I can see that it might not have peacefully coexisted with the self-sacrificing asceticism of the new East European Jewish settlers. The Bukharan community chose pleasure over ideology and seemed out of tune with history.

This idyllic image of food plenty and generous hospitality was certainly true at times, but Zion's memoir offers a rather different take, as it often recounts the petty disputes, disagreements and struggles that kept the family separated between Samarkand and Jerusalem for over a decade. The family strife only ended when Abraham divorced Uzbak, his second wife (and Batya-Hannah's mother), and married for the third time. Abraham's third bride was Rachel Douek, a young Jewish woman originally from Aleppo in Syria.[5] Zion doesn't comment on the reasons behind Abraham's decision to divorce Uzbak – nor does he mention his mother Tova, although she still lived nearby in Jerusalem – but the family rifts could have been a decisive factor. Throughout his memoir, Zion described Abraham as a man guided by his passions, not by reason or tradition. This third marriage could simply be another expression of Abraham's impulsive and self-centred character. Despite Zion's harsh views of his father, it seems that this time the family accepted the decisions of the sixty-year-old patriarch more peacefully.

Rachel brought the delicate flavours of her hometown and the wider Ottoman world into the Asheroff house. Aleppo's cuisine excelled at stuffing and rolling. Every vegetable, animal and leaf were stuffed with a delicate mixture of rice, meat and herbs. The careful attention of the cook drew rich and sophisticated flavours from even the humblest vegetables. In the courtyard vegetable garden, Rachel grew cardoon, or harshoof, a distant relative of the artichoke with no leaves and a tender stalk. She would stuff the stalks of harshoof with meat, and cook them in a lemony sauce. When Batya-Hannah and Zion came to Rachel and Abraham's house to celebrate Passover, they brought a large bowl of fresh fruit, as a sign of a new beginning, and shared the family's celebratory meal of stuffed harshoof and lamb roast.

## STUFFED HARSHOOF

Take 4–5 fresh stalks of harshoof. Wash them, trim off the dry parts and peel the stalks with a sharp knife. Halve each one lengthways and cut it into finger-long pieces. Boil the harshoof in salty water for 15 minutes and then drain them carefully. When they are cool, delicately open the stalks with a knife. Meanwhile, in a large bowl mix 200g of minced beef, 2 tablespoons of matzo meal or breadcrumbs, 4 tablespoons of chopped coriander and season with salt and pepper. Lightly beat 1 egg, and add half of it to the meat mixture (keep the rest). Using the palm of your hand, make long patties of meat and stuff each harshoof stalk with a patty. Dip the stuffed harshoof in the remainder of the beaten egg, then dust them lightly with flour or fine matzo meal. Heat 4–5 tablespoons of olive oil in a pan and fry the harshoof on each side until golden. Place the fried harshoof on a plate. Make a runny sauce with 3 peeled and chopped tomatoes (or 3–4 tablespoons of tinned tomato pulp, or you can leave out the tomatoes altogether), 1 cup (240ml) of water, the juice of ½ a lemon, some parsley leaves and a little salt and sugar to taste. Bring to the boil over a medium heat and then lower the heat, add the fried harshoof and simmer for 20 minutes, adding some more water if needed.

WHILE ZION, BATYA-HANNAH AND THEIR CHILDREN SETTLED down to their new life in Jerusalem, the Russian and Japanese empires were engaged in a war in the Pacific Ocean. After its expansion southwards, to Central Asia, the tsarist empire had ambitions further the east, clashing with Japan's interests. The

Manchurian peninsula where the conflict took place might have seemed distant from Palestine, but the echoes of war arrived strong and clear in Samarkand.

The war did not end in a quick Russian victory, as Tsar Nicholas II had expected. Rather, the Russians suffered a humiliating defeat which enhanced the popular discontent and led to widespread strikes, protests and, eventually, to the 1905 revolution.[6] Across the Russian Empire, social unrest brought trade to a stop. For Zion, whose income depended on trade between Russian and Ottoman lands, these were worrying developments. Sooner than he had planned or wished, he rushed back to Samarkand to save the family's business. Batya-Hannah, who was expecting a baby, remained in Jerusalem with the children. As the first Asheroff child born in Jerusalem, the baby was named Zvia, after the gazelle that symbolizes the land of Israel.

Batya-Hannah must have been happy to stay behind in the city she grew up in. She could finally enjoy the elegant house that her husband worked hard to finance. Her children went to local schools and learned Hebrew and Arabic. Living in Jerusalem also brought back childhood memories of local food: warm pitta bread, marinated olives, and slices of aubergine paired with a patty of minced meat in a thick tomato sauce. A typical Judaeo-Spanish preparation, it found its way into culinary traditions all over the Ottoman Mediterranean, and also to Batya-Hannah's kitchen.

# STUFFED AUBERGINES

Preheat the oven to 170°C (gas mark 3). Season 500g of minced beef with salt, pepper and chopped parsley. Take 2 large aubergines and cut them into 2cm slices. With a knife, hollow out one side of each slice so it's like a shallow bowl and fill the well with a patty of the minced meat. Dust the slices with flour and heat some olive oil in a pan. Fry the patties carefully on both sides until golden. In a large shallow ovenproof pot with a lid, fry 1 finely chopped onion until it's golden. Add 2 cups (500ml) of crushed tomatoes (fresh or canned), 2 garlic cloves, 1 cup (240ml) of water and season with salt and pepper. Cook the sauce for 15 minutes. Carefully place the fried patties in the sauce, cover the pot with the lid and cook in the oven for 1 hour, or until the aubergines are soft. Serve on top of white long-grain rice.

Abraham and Rachel shared the house with Batya-Hannah and her children, as well as with the family of Abraham's second son, Eliahu-Zvi, who decided to set up a dairy farm. Their house's location, close to green pastures, seemed ideal. In Samarkand, every family kept livestock to provide milk for home-made butter, yoghurt and cheese, but in Jerusalem this was unusual, with only a few able to afford to keep animals. People usually bought milk and cheese from the nearby Arab villages. Eliahu-Zvi bought a couple of Dutch cows that provided plenty of fresh milk that the family could eat and sell. In the spring, they made kaimak from the rich sweet milk. Kaimak, a Samarkandi version of slightly fermented clotted cream, was the perfect ingredient for a light, airy cheesecake, like this recipe that sneaked into the family's culinary repertoire. Baked desserts are almost unknown in traditional Samarkandi cuisine. Perhaps the cake was introduced from Aleppo by Rachel, or encountered by Abraham and Zion on one of their visits to Istanbul. Whatever its origin, it was adopted as a favourite dessert, to be served with sweet preserved Samarkandi apricots.

# CHEESECAKE

Grease a 20cm cake tin with butter and preheat the oven to 170°C (gas mark 3). Separate 3 eggs and whisk the egg whites, gradually adding 5 tablespoons (75g) of sugar, until they form stiff peaks. Beat the egg yolks with 1 tablespoon (15g) of sugar until they are light and creamy. Fold the egg whites into the yolks mixture, then gently fold in the juice and zest of 1 lemon. Divide the egg mixture into a third and two-thirds. Make the base of the cake by folding 40g of sifted flour into the third of the egg mixture, pour into the prepared tin and bake it in the oven for 10 minutes. Whisk 500g of kaimak (or, in its absence, you could use clotted cream or full-fat Greek yoghurt) until it is smooth and soft. Gently fold the remainder of the egg mixture into the whipped kaimak. Remove the cake base from the oven and spread the creamy egg mixture evenly on top. Return to the oven for 30–35 minutes or until the cake is set. Leave to cool before serving.

IN THE SUMMER, THE WOMEN PREPARED A YOGHURT-LIKE fermented drink inspired by Central Asian kumis, typically made of the fermented milk of a mare. Since this was not strictly kosher, in Jerusalem they used cow's milk instead. Similar in taste to the Turkish kefir, kumis was a little sweeter and ever so slightly alcoholic, a perfect refresher for hot days. In the winter, they churned creamy salted butter and prepared a pure clarified butter that could keep fresh for months. In Samarkand, this was added to hot tea, but Abraham's guests in Jerusalem failed to appreciate it.

It is perhaps unsurprising then that the dairy farm was hardly enough to sustain the extended Asheroff family. They still largely depended on the income that Zion sent from Samarkand. But the war and the revolution left Zion stranded in Samarkand, and Batya-Hannah had not heard any news from him. She could not rely on help from the rest of the family, who were also struggling to stay afloat. She sold her expensive suzani embroideries and precious rugs to raise money, but it was not enough. She took loans from her husband's friends in town, but still had hardly enough to feed her elder children and her newborn daughter. Once again, the only solution seemed to be to take to the road and return to Samarkand. She got tickets for a Russian sailing boat and set off with her children. Packing up her family and travelling back to Central Asia was not heroic or adventurous.

She was a confident and practiced traveller. In Istanbul, she sent Zion a telegram to tell him that they were on their way, and not long afterwards the family was reunited in Samarkand.

As a migrant, I am used to strangers asking where I am from. Even when I tell them that 'I live here', they then ask, 'Yes, but where are you *really* from?' This sometimes seems like a silent accusation of the undefined crime of not-belonging, but I also understand that pinning down a person to a place can be an indispensable part of getting to know them. If I could have addressed this question to Batya-Hannah, would her reply have been Jerusalem or Samarkand? Did she see herself as part of the Russian Empire, or the Ottoman one? Perhaps the meaning of the question would escape her. She spent her life between two cities, and seemed just as comfortable in her family home as on the road across the desert, on a boat passing through the Istanbul straits, or onboard a Russian train. Travelling was not heroic or adventurous, it was a normal part of her life.

Batya-Hannah and Zion were both descendants of generations of travelling merchants, and their sense of identity was lodged in this mobile community. Their families, the Asheroffs and Fuzailoffs, were used to travel. They were interconnected by multiple marriages and business partnerships, and kept in close touch even through distance, and long periods of tension and disagreement. Sometimes, these bonds were reinforced by tragedy. In 1912, Zion's younger brother Eliahu-Zvi, was shot dead by a cattle thief. After reading a letter from his heartbroken father, Zion decided to put all their previous disagreements behind them, to make amends. Not long afterwards, Abraham died too, and Zion's mother Tova followed in 1916. Going back to Jerusalem would no longer mean going back home: the square stone house with its lemon-scented patio would still be there, but his family and the feasts they hosted would be forever different.

The question of identity may not have troubled Zion and his wife, but the early decades of the twentieth century soon forced them to choose their allegiance. When the First World War broke out, Batya-Hannah and Zion discovered that they could no longer return to Jerusalem – as Russian subjects they were considered enemy aliens. Bukharan and Samarkandi families in Jerusalem were also forced to choose: take up Ottoman nationality and join the army, or leave. Most men escaped abroad, some leaving behind women and children in poverty. The Bukharan Quarter, and the Asheroff house, were emptied of their inhabitants and left deserted, unkempt and forgotten. The Asheroff widows and their children lived on, waiting for the tide to turn.

# Chapter 3

# ZOULAY ASHEROFF IN SAMARKAND, 1908–1924

IN LATE 1905, BATYA-HANNAH AND HER CHILDREN LEFT Jerusalem and were reunited with Zion in Samarkand. In his memoir, Zion related how, slowly, the family regathered the fragments of their life. He started trading again and bought another house in Samarkand, large enough to accommodate his expanding family. The house had high ceilings, sparse windows and little furniture apart from beautifully embroidered rugs and suzani textiles with elaborate patterns of pomegranates and flowers. The rooms surrounded a large patio, where the whole family would meet, eat and socialize. Unlike Muslim houses, there were no separate courtyards for men and women, but instead a single courtyard with peach and apricot trees that abounded with ripe fruit in the summer. In their shade, the family kept hens and goats for fresh eggs and milk. In summertime, they dried fresh apricots, peaches, tomatoes and melons on wooden trays for the cold days of winter, as I saw when walking in the streets of Samarkand more than a century later. It was a place of nourishment and plenty.

Hananya, Zion and Batya-Hannah's eldest son, was eleven when the family returned to Samarkand. By then, he had already travelled across Asia and accompanied his father on business trips to Moscow. Like his father, he also wrote a memoir, in which I read about his cosmopolitan and adventurous life.[1] From a young age, he experienced Samarkand as a crossroads of cultures: Russian and Muslim, imperial and local. He studied mathematics, German, English and Russian in a secular gymnasium, a secondary school that prepared its pupils for university studies. Yet, instead of attending university, after graduation Hananya started working at his father's fabric shop. In the evenings, he read any book that he could get his hands on. He was attracted by the Jadid reformist movement that erupted in the city, seeking to adapt Islamic education and traditions to modern times, and hoped to emulate their vision for the Jewish community.[2] Like many young reformers of his generation in Samarkand, he believed in free secular education, equal rights for women, and state-funded social welfare and healthcare. He loved music and theatre, and counted Muslim, Russian and Jewish boys among his friends. He wanted to be an international merchant like his father, but he also had aspirations to become a public figure, a leader.

In 1912, at eighteen, Hananya married his first cousin, Zoulay Fuzailoff. Zoulay was the daughter of Yohanan Fuzailoff, Batya-Hannah's brother and Zion's business partner and friend. Perhaps the wedding was arranged by the two families. In any case, the wedding party hardly reflected Hananya's reformist beliefs. Like her mother and mother-in-law, at her wedding Zoulay wore a traditional bright green silk paranji that covered her face and restricted her movement. Muslim women in Samarkand wore this garment whenever they left the house, but Jewish women were not required to.

The paranji was beautifully crafted of jacquard silk, lined with ikat-patterned cotton and finished with colourful ribbons, but it was not a garment for those seen as progressive, modern women.

I have discovered little about Zoulay. Unlike her husband, she left behind no diary, no letters; nothing survived but her paranji, a few photographs and her recipes, which her daughter, my grandmother Shulamit, taught me. Though I cannot be sure if Zoulay and Hananya's wedding was a union of love or convenience, her importance in my life is unquestionable. Through her recipes she was the source of so many of the flavours that shaped my childhood. They are not a set of instructions. They are a memory, an intuition; I emulate her methods in my own kitchen. By cooking the food she used to make, I can try to imagine what kind of woman she was, what kind of life she lived.

Zoulay never went to school, because her father did not believe that women should get an education. I am not sure if she could read and write. When she grew up, at least until the Bolshevik Revolution of 1917 imposed new laws of gender equality, Samarkandi women were rarely educated out of the home.[3] Yet even with these restrictions, Hananya's sisters all studied at home and could read and write in at least two languages. Zoulay's life was largely confined to the walls of her family home: first her father's and then her husband's. Her name meant 'brilliant beauty' in Persian (Farsi), but in the few photographs we have of her, I see a timid, reserved woman, with a beaky nose and slightly melancholic look. She owned beautiful, precious things made with talent and skill: long silk frocks in bright shades of green and yellow, and necklaces of silver beads that tinkled as she walked. But at home, her usual outfit was a simple dress and a practical apron. Samarkandi families often used a *kaybanu*, a professional cook who helped prepare larger meals and celebrations. Batya-Hannah certainly had one – Zion even sponsored her travel permit to Palestine in 1924 – but Zoulay had to manage mostly alone.

In Samarkand then – and now – men and women occupied different spaces, but it seems to me that Hananya and Zoulay almost lived in different times too. She was a woman of the past, and he wanted to become a man of the future. He was outgoing and well educated, she was shy and almost illiterate; he was a confident womanizer, she was a calm and hard-working wife and mother; he travelled the world, she left her native Samarkand only once, never to return.

It's easy to imagine Zoulay sitting under the vine canopy in the patio of a whitewashed building, kneading dough and chopping vegetables in the shade. At home, she had everything she needed to prepare magnificent meals. In the cool pantry, the family kept large glass bottles of home-made wine and arak, chunks of yellow butter and buckets of fresh cheese. Daily supplies were delivered from the local market and the Jewish butcher. But the outside world, the streets lined with water canals, the chai-khana under the mulberry trees in the square, the market and the monumental square of the Registan, was out of her reach. Perhaps, she was never particularly keen to reach them, content with the restricted, domestic space she had occupied since childhood.

Zoulay's cooking changed from season to season, because the house had two kitchens: a summer outdoor kitchen with a hot tandoor oven, and an indoor winter kitchen, which was essentially a small dark room with a clay hearth. Every morning, she would feed the oven in the courtyard with new wood to keep the temperature hot without actually lighting a fire. The wood would slowly burn into coal, which she expertly spread around the round clay oven. On a large metal plate set inside the oven she quickly baked thin crisp noni-tokhi, decorated with pin-stamps of flowers or stars of David. She baked small triangular pastries called bichak, filled with pumpkin paste, and goshgidja – round balls filled with onion and meat. These tiny delicate mouthfuls, sprinkled with black nigella or cumin seeds, were served piping hot, crisp and soft, burning the tongue of the impatient eater. They were eaten almost without noticing, slipping into the mouth, washed down with a glass of arak or wine.

## GOSHGIDJA

Mix 1 cup (140g) of flour, 1 egg yolk, 1 tablespoon of oil, 1 tablespoon of water, ½ teaspoon of dried yeast and ½ teaspoon of salt in a bowl to form a smooth dough, then cover it and let it rest for 1 hour. Preheat the oven to 180°C (gas mark 4). In a saucepan, saute 1 finely chopped onion with some oil until it's golden. Allow it to cool and then mix with 250g of finely chopped or minced lamb. Now the dough has rested, place it on a lightly floured surface and roll it out 3mm thick and cut out circles 6cm in diameter. Place a teaspoonful of stuffing in the centre of each circle, and gather up the edges towards the centre to close. Place the parcels on a lightly oiled baking sheet with their seams facing down, and brush the tops with some oil. Sprinkle with nigella or sesame seeds, and bake for 15 minutes or until they're golden.

Zoulay kept her most elaborate dishes for holidays; she used to say that they lost their appeal if they were cooked and eaten every day. Their rarity endowed them with a particular delight, a touch of the unattainable. Osh-palao was one such dish, reserved for major festivities. Even the wealthiest Samarkandis did not eat palao every day, but just once a week, on a Friday night, as a special treat for the Shabbat dinner. But when I was a little girl and visiting my grandma Shulamit, she would, in her words, 'waste' the rarefied osh-palao on midweek dinners. It was how she showed me her love.

As a child, eating osh-palao made me feel nostalgic for a place I would visit only years later, as the flavours and scents took me straight to my ancestral city on the Silk Road, a city that was admired by travellers and faraway poets for centuries. For me, Samarkand is more than an exotic destination; it was the birthplace of the woman whose food I grew up with. When I eventually went to the city, I saw osh-palao in every restaurant. It was the main course in every meal I ate, in one version or another, but it was not exactly the festive dish I had known from my grandmother's kitchen. The ubiquitous preparation was now called plov in the Russian manner – palao is apparently the more common Tajik or Afghan pronunciation, but there are many local versions – and was prepared exclusively by men, in a large metal pot called a *kazan* which was placed on an open fire outdoors. At the market I saw piles of pre-cut thin strips of yellow and orange carrots, ready to facilitate the preparation of plov at home. When I was invited to a family feast at a local Samarkandi home, we shared a large tray of plov, sprinkled with sweet and sour barberries. Although I was a guest in a foreign city, I did not feel out of place. Through my great-grandmother's recipes, Samarkand and its flavours have already become a part of me.

# OSH-PALAO

Warm 2 tablespoons of mutton fat (or vegetable oil) in a large metal pot over the fire (or in a heavy bottomed saucepan on the stove), and fry 300g of lamb diced into 3–4cm cubes, turning them until they are cooked on all sides. Remove the meat from the pan. Wash and drain 2 cups (400g) of rice. In separate bowls, soak 1 cup (150g) of raisins (preferably Uzbek) and barberries and 1 cup (150g) of peeled almonds in hot water. In the meantime, use the pan you cooked the lamb in to sauté 2 thinly sliced onions until they turn golden. Return the meat to the pan, and cover with 8 large carrots cut into thin strips. Add a little water, cover and cook for 5 minutes. Do not stir. Add the rice on top of the carrots, and season with salt. Drain the raisins, barberries and almonds and place them in separate mounds on top of the rice. Pour boiling water on top of the rice until it covers it by 2cm. Simmer for about 10 minutes, or until the rice has absorbed most of the water, then cover the pan with a clean tea towel and a lid, and steam for 20 minutes on a very low heat. Turn off the heat and let the rice rest for 10 minutes. Serve the rice on a large sharing plate, topped with the meat, carrots and dried fruit.

THE AMU DARYA RIVER VALLEY WHERE SAMARKAND LIES has always been fertile ground for the cultivation of rice, as the river provides plenty of water to soak the delicate plants. But until the Soviet regime industrialized local agriculture, rice was considered a luxury in comparison to cheaper wheat or millet. Rice featured in some of Zoulay's most memorable recipes. She would use a particular kind of local rice, which would remain plump and firm after cooking, never becoming too dry or sticky. The most prestigious local grain is devzira, an ancient and almost extinct variety of rice that has to be fermented in water for months before use; perhaps that is the rice that Zoulay used to cook with, instead of the more common basmati rice I use today. Some of the rice dishes that she used to make have also disappeared from the restaurants and food stalls of modern Uzbekistan, where plov now reigns unchallenged, but I can trace their presence in the memories of migrants and diaspora communities in Israel, New York and Russia. Maybe they live only in the kitchens of those families who left the city generations ago.

One of these vanishing dishes is the oshi-bakhsh, which Zoulay only prepared on special occasions. It a green rice dish full of chopped coriander and mint, dotted with tiny cubes of lamb and liver, and cooked with enough fat to form a crunchy layer at the bottom of the pot. For Jewish New Year's Eve, it was served with tangy red pomegranate seeds to freshen up its flavour, and it was also used as a stuffing for chicken, quinces and apples, the seasonal fruit of the autumn. It is my favourite dish from Zoulay's repertoire, at once earthy and fresh, crisp and fragrant. But during my stay in Samarkand, I could not find it anywhere.

# OSHI-BAKHSH

In a large pot, place 500g of lamb and 100g of fresh liver, both chopped into small cubes, with 80ml of lamb tail fat (or vegetable oil) and cover it all with water. Bring the pan to a boil and stir well. Finely chop 2 large bunches of coriander – the more the better – and a smaller bunch of mint. Add the herbs to the boiling meat mixture, season with salt and mix thoroughly. Next add 2 cups (400g) of washed basmati rice and stir again. Add enough water to cover the rice and bring back to a boil. When it is boiling well, cover the pot with a clean cloth and a lid, and steam over a low heat for 20 minutes or until the rice is fluffy. Serve with a squeeze of fresh lemon juice or sprinkle pomegranate seeds and a side of fresh tomato and cucumber salad.

IN THE YEARS FOLLOWING THEIR MARRIAGE, HANANYA continued to travel, back and forth, to Jerusalem, to Moscow, to Odessa. The new railway network had transformed what had been a gruelling caravan trip lasting a month into a comfortable journey of only a week. Dressed in elegant suits and as fluent in Russian as he was in Judaeo-Tajik, Hananya felt at home in the tsarist empire. He moved easily through it with no need of passports or permits. Even his Jewishness, which in those days often put limits on one's freedom of movement, did not seem to restrict his ambitions.

Zoulay was a dedicated cook, but her skills were constantly measured and assessed by Hananya. Every evening, he expected to eat well, in a beautiful room, surrounded by interesting people, whom he would usually invite without informing his wife. When he returned home, he would enter the dining room, lit with precious wax candles and brightly coloured silk cushions, take his seat at the head of the low table and wait. In the freezing winter months, Zoulay's cooking brought out the warm, earthy flavours of the vegetables in her garden in her sirkaniz, a colourful rice dish decorated with cubes of deep red beetroot, bright orange carrots and tender chickpeas. When the large sharing plate of rice was set at the heart of the table, she ceremoniously poured hot lamb fat infused with garlic over it and sprinkled fresh dill on top, before retiring to the kitchen and letting Hananya serve his guests, all of whom were men. In his own household, there was not a trace of the progressive approach to women's rights and equality that he promoted so enthusiastically in public.

## SIRKANIZ

Overnight, soak 1 cup (150g) of dried chickpeas in 2 litres of water with 1 teaspoon of baking soda. The next day, wash the chickpeas and boil them in fresh water until they are tender. Drain the cooked chickpeas and remove their skins. In a large pan, seal 300g of fatty lamb cubes (you can leave this out if you want) in ½ cup (120ml) of vegetable oil or lamb tail fat. Add the chickpeas and finely chopped generous bunches of coriander and dill (about 50g each) to the warm oil (and lamb cubes if you're using them) and mix well. Season with salt and pepper. Add 1½ cups (300g) of washed basmati rice and 500ml water, or enough to cover the rice. Do not stir. Cook this over a high heat for 15 minutes and then lower the heat, cover the saucepan with a clean cloth and lid and steam for a further 20 minutes. Meanwhile, boil 3 large beetroots and 3 large carrots until they are tender. Peel and cut the cooked vegetables into long strips about 1cm thick. When the rice and vegetables are ready, gently heat 50ml of sesame oil or mutton fat in a small saucepan. Place 2 chopped garlic cloves in a small bowl, and pour the warmed oil or fat over it. Serve the sirkaniz rice on a large plate, scatter it with the beetroots and carrots and some freshly chopped dill, then pour the garlic infusion on top.

IN THE COURTYARD OF THE ASHEROFF HOUSE, THERE WAS A vine that created a shaded canopy over the outdoor dining area and flavoured the household's food and drink all year long. According to legend, the ancient peoples of Samarkand, the Sugdians, taught the Chinese how to ferment grape juice instead of rice. Grapes have long been an indispensable part of the local culinary heritage. The fertile soil gave them succulence and sweetness, which produced a ruby-coloured wine with a deep, fruity aroma. But the Muslim emirs banned the production and consumption of alcohol, and it was only after the Russian occupation that winemaking started to thrive in Samarkand.

By the First World War, many Samarkandi Jews were drinking wine, vodka and other spirits with their meals. Wine is an inseparable part of the Jewish culture, the only drink in the Bible that has its own unique blessing. Every autumn, Hananya would pick the ripe grapes and make wine, which he would keep in huge glass jars in shaded corners of the house. They would periodically explode from the pressure of fermentation, to the children's fear and delight. Hananya's real passion was arak, however, and he made the twice-distilled alcoholic drink with grape pomace and anise, whose aroma would fill the house with freshness.

On autumnal Fridays, Zoulay would use fresh plump grapes to prepare khalti-sevo, a rice dish with dried and fresh fruit cooked overnight and served exclusively for Saturday lunch. She stuffed an old linen bag with rice, chopped apples, quinces and grapes, and then immersed it in a fruity beef broth inside a clay pot, where it slow-cooked in the tandoor for hours. The next day, she would extract the scented, purple rice from its wrapping and tip it into a serving bowl, amidst a cloud of steam.

Cooking in a linen bag was a special technique, perhaps typical of the Jewish community of Samarkand and less commonly used elsewhere. It allowed the rice to cook slowly in a flavoursome sauce, without losing its fine texture. In my kitchen today, I keep one of Zoulay's stained brown bags, their quality undiminished by decades of use. But after Zoulay's death, the recipe for khalti-sevo was lost: none of her descendants knew how to cook it. All I could garner from the recollections of her grandchildren was a memory of the sweet and tangy purple-brown rice, a perfect meal for colder days.

In the spring, when vine leaves were tender and fresh, Zoulay would stuff them delicately with rice and coriander. In her *Book of Jewish Food*, food anthropologist Claudia Roden suggested that stuffed vegetables were introduced to Central Asia by the envoys who came from Jerusalem to teach the locals the wisdom of the Bible, but stuffed vine leaves – or cabbage leaves in the winter – are a common presence in many parts of the world.[4] Zoulay's recipe, which cooks the stuffed vine leaves in a lemony sauce with chickpeas and fresh herbs, seems unusual because lemons were not particularly common in Samarkand before the Soviets started cultivating them in the 1930s. Like the Turkish recipes, the vine leaves were filled with a rice mixture, but the flavours were tangy and sour, rather than sweetish, because no dried fruit was used. I know that Hananya was also passionate about his garden, so he might have experimented with growing lemons there, as his grandfather and father had done in the courtyard of the Asheroffs' house in Jerusalem.

## STUFFED VINE LEAVES

Overnight, soak 1 cup (150g) of dried chickpeas in cold water (you can add 1 teaspoon of baking soda, which helps soften them). The next day, wash the chickpeas well, put them in a pot full of water and boil them until tender. While the chickpeas are cooking, soak 1 cup (200g) of basmati rice in hot water for an hour. Drain the rice, and put it in a bowl with 250g of minced beef or lamb, ½ cup (50g) of chopped parsley, ½ cup (50g) of chopped coriander, 2 tablespoons of olive oil and a pinch of grated nutmeg. Mix it all well, seasoning it with salt and pepper. Wash some 40 fresh, young whole vine leaves. Place a tablespoon of the rice and meat mix in the middle of each leaf, then fold the sides towards the centre and roll the bottom towards the top to make a tightly closed roll. Drain the cooked chickpeas, remove their skins, and place them in a large ovenproof pot. Add the juice of 2 large lemons to the chickpeas, and arrange the stuffed vine leaves snugly on top. Place a plate upside down on top of the vine leaves, and pour boiling water over, arriving at the top layer. Cook for 15 minutes over medium heat. Preheat the oven to 170°C (gas mark 3). Remove the plate, cover the pot with the lid, put it in the oven and bake for 30 minutes.

ON MY DESK, I SPREAD OUT THE THICK YELLOWING SHEETS of Hananya's memoir, filled with lines of neat handwriting. It is only thirty-odd pages, recounting his youthful adventures in the self-important and confident tone of a man who knows he witnessed history's greatest events. Yet he never mentions Zoulay. He was concerned with leaving a legacy, a testimony, a story of his life, but did not consider her a part of it. He wasn't alone in placing Zoulay at the margins. Her niece, Edna, also remembers her as a submissive and modest woman, almost vanishing into the background of his active life. Yet my grandmother Shulamit – Zoulay's daughter – always told me that Zoulay knew that, along with the flavours and scents of her food, she would not be forgotten.

Reading Hananya's Hebrew script, I found myself searching for an explanation of how the family adapted to the First World War.

Although Zion felt that the war cut his ties with Jerusalem once and for all, his son Hananya seemed, initially at least, indifferent to the collapse of the European peace. The distant battles between European empires was foreign to his daily routine, and he continued to travel to Moscow to buy embroidered textiles and Russian lace and sell exquisite Atlas silk. He went with his Muscovite friends to the cinema, to the theatre and to elegant restaurants. But slowly, obstacles emerged. When the Russian colonial regime wanted to curb the liberties granted to the local population by enforcing military conscription, he managed to buy his way out of the army. Soon, he would discover that even a bon-vivant cosmopolitan merchant could find himself in the middle of a revolution.

Signs of unrest started to manifest themselves closer to the Asheroffs' home. In 1916, thousands of peasants in the vast lands of Uzbekistan, Tajikistan and Kazakhstan who moved to revolt against tsarist domination were killed by the Russian army. Others lost their land and sought refuge in China.[5] In the winter of 1917, Hananya sat in the warm living room of the Muscovite owner of a textile factory with whom he had just concluded a successful deal. Earlier that afternoon, he had witnessed thousands of workers taking to the streets of Moscow, protesting against the government. Armed with red flags and posters, they called for freedom, peace, land and bread. He congratulated his host for the relative peacefulness of the revolution, which he hoped would announce a new democratic and prosperous era for Russia. The local man thought otherwise: 'I assure you that the streets will soon be washed in red.'

Later that night, when he discovered that Tsar Nicholas II had been forced to abdicate, Hananya rushed home to Samarkand. By the time he reached Central Asia, chaos ruled. As the cotton trade came to a halt and commercial routes became unsafe, Samarkand succumbed to poverty and hunger, which the Bolshevik administration hoped to alleviate by forcing the population to undertake agricultural labour on newly established collective farms.[6] Before these plans could be realized, the disruption to trade risked causing a long-term economic crisis in the city.

Hananya's business stumbled, too, when the transfer of goods across Russia became too dangerous, but during the commercial slowdown he discovered a passion for public affairs. Unsurprisingly, his main interest was food: Hananya's first step as a political activist was to set up a Jewish cooperative food bank. He bought large bags of flour and rice, slabs of fresh butter and sacks of potatoes, and secured from local farmers a supply of carrots, beetroots, onions, garlic and chickpeas, dried fruit and fresh herbs. An armed man guarded the stock day and night. Each family contributed according to its means and received sufficient supplies for modest and nourishing meals. Soon, only members of the cooperative had enough food to survive, while the rest of Samarkand's residents started to feel the sting of hunger.

The Bolsheviks eventually shut down the food bank, but by that point Hananya's name had been noted by higher political echelons as a young and ambitious member of the Jewish community who sported some socialist sympathies. That sufficed to appoint him as vice commissar of the city council. He was put in charge of trade: all goods that entered or left the city had to carry his authorization. In practice, his main responsibility was to secure food supplies for the city's population and for the crowded military camp stationed in its outskirts. When the army regularly looted then squandered the little food that was left to local residents, the redistribution of provisions could determine who would survive and who would starve. The commissar, an illiterate railway worker, was glad to leave such delicate business in Hananya's hands, yet reminded him that in case of disagreement, he had a gun and knew how to use it.

Cooking in Samarkand after the revolution was an act of defiance against political instability. The actual arrival of the Bolsheviks, in 1922, did nothing to mitigate the local destitution.[7] Yet Samarkandi cuisine adapted well to hard times, as courtyards and family orchards proved an indispensable source of food. Every house in the Jewish Mahalla had its own little vegetable garden, a constant source of nourishment and comfort. Zoulay could count on the Asheroff orchard: even when food was scarce she could stuff yellow quinces from her tree with rice and coriander and roast them until they turned pinkish red. But the outside world increasingly crept through the walls and into her life.

## STUFFED QUINCES

Take 6 smooth, large, yellow quinces and wash them well. Make the stuffing by mixing 50g of minced lamb with 2 tablespoons (20g) of finely chopped coriander, 1 tablespoon (10g) of finely chopped mint leaves, 2 tablespoons (30ml) of oil (or 20g lamb's fat) and a pinch of salt. Place the mixture in a small saucepan with ½ cup (120ml) of water and cook for 10 minutes. Take the pan off the heat and add ½ cup (100g) of washed basmati rice. Cut off the top of the quinces and put them aside. Using a sharp knife or a melon spoon, hollow out the quinces and remove all the seeds. Fill the quinces with the stuffing, and put the tops back on them. Place the quinces snugly in a pan, and sprinkle them with 4 tablespoons of brown sugar. Add 2 cups (500ml) of vegetable or chicken stock, 3 tablespoons (45ml) of oil and a squeeze of fresh lemon juice. Cook over a medium-low heat for 2 hours, or until the quinces are soft and the rice is cooked. While they are cooking, every now and then, wet the quinces' stuffing with a tablespoon of the sauce.

FOOD, FOOD, FOOD. READING HANANYA'S DIARY, IT SEEMS to me that this was all he could think about. How to make sure that his family and his community had enough to eat. It was not an easy task, competing for provisions not only with other Samarkandi residents, but also with the Red Army and the gangs of thieves that frequently raided shops and houses. Samarkand was initially ruled by the Bolsheviks through local leaders, enthusiastic young reformists who hoped the new era would transform the region. These were Hananya's old allies, and at first he shared their reformist visions. Yet they set up a governing committee that instituted a new tax, confiscating 50 per cent of all produce in Samarkand. It was a harsh blow for a starving city. Hananya and a couple of friends decided to deal with the situation in their own way: they bribed a member of the governing committee, hoping that he would help to cancel the decree. The man took the money and promptly sent them all to prison. Hananya was released a few days later, but after this episode, he was out of favour with the revolutionary regime.

Zion, Hananya's father, was unaware of his political activities. In his diary, he recounts how one night he returned home late – and slightly inebriated – after a long dinner party with friends, only to be woken up by four men searching for his son. Wary of their intentions, he instructed Hananya to slip out of his room, into the garden, and hide in the stream in the far end of the yard. When the visitors asked Zion to go and look for his son, he replied, 'He is a grown man and he won't tell me where he goes.' In the morning, Hananya was no longer at home. Zion assumed that he must have jumped over the high walls that surrounded the garden and headed to one of the orchards outside the city. He returned the following day, hoping that the danger was over.

Yet not a week had passed when there was another knock on the door, and a member of the Russian military accompanied by a sentry told Zion that if he could not find Hananya, they would imprison his younger sons instead, and, eventually, his own life would be at stake. It was a Jewish friend, a Russian translator, who persuaded Zion to turn Hananya over to the police, promising that he would only be questioned and not imprisoned. Before Zion could make up his mind, a few days later, in the middle of the Shabbat dinner, the policemen returned to the Asheroff home. They arrested Hananya and sent him to prison in Tashkent, along with the translator friend who had promised Zion that all would be well.

The Tashkent prison, located in the city's fortress, was famed for breaking people's bodies and spirit. It was over-crowded, filled with political prisoners who awaited their turn in front of the firing squad in the main court. 'All the gates are locked, except for those of the tears,' wrote Zion of the endless wails of the prisoners, matched only by the crying and moaning of their families outside. The prison was a place of suffering, but mostly of uncertainty. In his diary, Hananya recalls that a brigade of Mensheviks, the anti-Leninist Russian left-wing social democrats, took over the Bolshevik prison one winter day. Their leader, Kolissov, liberated all the bourgeois merchants, Hananya included. Luckily, Hananya and a friend managed to find a horse and rode back to Samarkand before the Bolsheviks could imprison him again.

There is an alternative account of Hananya's prison escape, told to me by my grandmother Shulamit, which focuses on Batya-Hannah, Hananya's mother, who apparently travelled all the way from Samarkand to the Tashkent prison dressed as a man. She bribed a guard with a bottle of precious home-made arak and got her son released. It would be a curious story to invent, and it shows Batya-Hannah to be an unusually powerful and independent woman. Even if it is entirely fictitious, it is compelling. She had travelled alone with young children all the way from Jerusalem to Samarkand. Why not imagine her negotiating her son's liberation in Tashkent? And Hananya regaining his freedom thanks to a bottle of his own arak seems only just.

When Hananya returned to Samarkand, his friends and family roasted a whole lamb to welcome him home. In times of such hardship, it was a grand gesture. The courtyard would have been filled with people, the men and women sitting together, gathering around the turning spit, eating raisins and melon before the meat was served. A whole lamb was an exceptional, almost frivolous treat, but this sacrificial lamb was, perhaps, a mark of a changing tide. Soon afterwards, trade was re-instituted across the newly minted Soviet Union, the shops reopened in Samarkand and the city seemed to return to its usual rhythm. Hananya still saw his future there. He set up a theatre and a library where young people could listen to music, drink tea and eat together. His textile business was successful enough to allow the family to contemplate the marriage of his younger siblings.

In his memoir, Zion wrote that this time of uncertainty generated in him a firm conviction that the family must leave Samarkand. Travelling on the usual route from Samarkand to Jerusalem became harder and harder as the Soviets and the British both started to control migration. Two options presented themselves to the Asheroff family: the first was to travel by train and boat via Odessa, and the second was a long camel caravan route via Mashad in Iran. Both required money, documentation, permits, passports and visas that were increasingly hard to get. Hananya wrote that to help his father, he decided to move to Moscow with Zoulay and their children, and to open a travel agency that could provide travel permits for his family and friends.

Zion already had a Russian passport, but it could not guarantee his family's way out of the country. In his memoir, he wrote that he needed a foreign passport. He did not mention *which* passport he was hoping to get. The answer was among the family documents that Zion's granddaughter Edna showed me: her parents had entered Palestine with an Afghan passport, and they kept their Afghan citizenship until the 1960s. In his British Palestine immigration documents, Hananya is also marked as Afghan. It seems probable that Zion and Batya-Hannah obtained Afghan passports too. In the 1920s, Afghan documents would have been a precious asset for Central Asians who wished to travel carefree in the Soviet Union and the British Empire. After its independence following the British defeat in the Anglo-Afghan War of 1919, Afghanistan was leading liberal reforms and strengthening its diplomatic relations with both London and Moscow.[8] Were the Asheroffs' passports genuine documents, issued through Hananya's connections at the Emirate of Bukhara's new embassy in Kabul, or false ones that he bought in Moscow? Either way, it is probable that none of the Asheroffs had ever made the 400km trip from Samarkand to Afghanistan, but the new citizenship allowed the family to leave Samarkand and set off on the long trip to Jerusalem.

In the spring of 1924, just before Samarkand officially became part of the new Soviet Republic of Uzbekistan, Zion, Batya-Hannah, their youngest daughter Penina and their grandchildren Daniel and Shoshana embarked on the Lloyd Triestino ship from Odessa to the port of Jaffa. The journey took them more than a month, with the last three weeks spent in the third class of the elegant ship. The ship stopped in ports in Romania and Turkey, but travellers were not allowed to disembark unless they had a visa. Without access to local markets and shops, Zion could not get provisions to cook food for his family. On board, he met Zionist representatives who offered to get off at the next port and buy him some food at the market. He asked for two bottles of cognac, a round bread, cucumbers, onion, garlic and all kinds of vegetables. The Zionists brought him the provisions and asked the captain to give Zion rice and oil from the ship's pantry. Every day, Zion cooked a dish of rice and vegetables in his third-class lodging. Every evening, he took it up to the first-class dining hall, where the captain, his assistant and the ship's doctor shared his meal and a glass of cognac.

While Hananya sent his eldest son, eleven-year-old Daniel, with his father to Jerusalem, he stayed behind in Moscow to settle the family's affairs and arrange travel documents for his siblings. When it became evident that the Asheroffs' era in Samarkand was coming to an end, Hananya, Zoulay and their younger children set off to join the rest of the family in Palestine. In their luggage, Hananya packed the roots of a young vine from his Samarkand vineyard, and took it with him to Jerusalem.

# Chapter 4

# THE ASHEROFF WOMEN IN JERUSALEM, 1927–1934

On a bright day in early April 1927, Zoulay, Hananya and their three young children set sail from Odessa. A desirable seaside resort designed by Italian architects, the beautiful city was recovering from a devastating famine. Despite this the golden beaches were full of elegantly dressed women, and the shops along the tree-lined avenues sold dresses and swimsuits of the latest fashion. Odessa famously attracted not only tourists but also artists, intellectuals and writers who made it the cultural capital of Ukraine.

Odessa was the main port of departure from the Soviet Union to Palestine. For travellers and migrants like the Asheroff family, it was an obvious stop en route out of Russia. Zion and his family had passed through this port three years earlier, and now came the turn of Hananya, Zoulay and the children. It had a large Jewish community, including many migrants from Samarkand and Bukhara, who welcomed newly arrived families into their homes until they were ready to continue their travels.

The Asheroffs reached Odessa by train from Moscow and embarked upon a passenger and cargo liner, usually operated by the Italian Lloyd Triestino shipping company, that would take them across the Black Sea to the Mediterranean. The trip could have taken up to three weeks, slowed down by many passport checks at each port on the way. The Asheroffs travelled in the second, or perhaps third class, packed in with travellers, the lucky few who had managed to obtain the much-desired travel certificates to leave the Soviet Union. Some were tourists, but many were secretly planning a new life elsewhere. Impoverished merchants, persecuted intellectuals, young families and political dissenters fled the Bolsheviks if they could and escaped to the Middle East, Europe or the Americas.[1]

The sights, the smells, the flavours were all new to Zoulay, refreshingly unfamiliar. She saw the blue expanse of the sea, gazed at the fishing villages and the mighty rocks, breathed in the salty breeze while standing on the deck. Many others in Zoulay's family had taken this route in the past: Hananya was a frequent traveller, and so were her father and her father-in-law, who had lived a life of constant mobility and had sailed across the Black Sea many times and along the eastern shore of the Mediterranean. But Zoulay had only travelled within the confines of the Russian Empire, from Samarkand to Moscow and now Odessa. In her new Russian passport she is pictured with her three youngest children, her beloved Michael, and her youngest Yehuda and Tamara, all squeezed together into one small photo, wearing European coats and hats. She was thirty-three years old and this was her first and last trip abroad.

In 1927, Haifa was a quickly expanding cosmopolitan trading city, with a new urban centre surrounded by small houses scattered over the green forests of Mount Carmel. The British governors of Palestine wanted to continue the Ottoman plan to develop the city into an important Mediterranean commercial hub, but the project would require time and money. When Zoulay's ship anchored at the port, it was still under construction. The dockers quickly unloaded the luggage and ushered the passengers to the shore. The family then hired a car and left the vast blue sea behind to head for Jerusalem, rattling and shaking all the way. A few hours later, they drove through the streets of the Bukharan Quarter and finally came to a stop in front of the Asheroff family home.

Much had changed in Jerusalem in the twenty years that Hananya had been in Samarkand, which he noted in his memoir with an air of slight disappointment. The dream of a garden city with modern architecture and natural plenty had been crushed by the First World War, leading to the neighbourhood's abandonment. It hadn't taken long for the once luxurious but now rather dilapidated houses to attract the attention of the city's new rulers, the British.

General Allenby's victorious entrance through the gates of Jerusalem in 1917 ended a millennium of Muslim control over the city and launched almost three decades of intense British interventions in both the territory and the lives of its inhabitants.[2] Surprisingly, perhaps, the British Empire's grandiose ambitions for Jerusalem resonated with the utopian vision of the wealthy families that had built the Bukharan Streets. The grand arched halls of the Yegudaioff palace, decorated with frescos of European landscapes and Jewish symbolism, became the setting for an elegant Passover seder for British Jewish soldiers, orchestrated by General Allenby, the Jewish jurist Norman Bentwich and the chief rabbi of Jerusalem. Another lavish feast was held there in Allenby's honour, with illustrious guests including governor Ronald Storrs and the future first president of Israel, Chaim Weizmann.[3] The ornate Bukharan palaces, equipped with modern comforts but reflecting a supposedly oriental aesthetic, surrounded by scented gardens, seemed to be the ideal background for celebrating the new 'civilized' Jerusalem, another jewel in the crown of the British Empire.

The Asheroff house was not particularly grand, but it was large enough to accommodate three generations of the family: Zion and Batya-Hannah, Hananya and Zoulay, and their children. Once again, they all celebrated Passover around the same table. The house was well built; it was a house that would stand for generations, or at least it seemed so then. It was certainly robust enough to survive the terrible earthquake that devastated many ancient buildings in Jerusalem, Nablus and Ramlah in July 1927 and claimed more than a hundred lives.[4] Hananya and Zoulay's first summer in Jerusalem was marred by the sad sights of a city in ruins, and the rising fear of another natural disaster. Maybe against this sense of collective anxiety, Hananya decided to plant the vine that he had brought from Samarkand. His grandchildren would, he hoped, enjoy its fruit.

Two more children were born to Zoulay and Hananya in Jerusalem. One of them was my grandmother, Shulamit, who boasted of her place of birth as a token of true belonging. Unlike her parents, she was not an immigrant. Her birth was an occasion for a feast, where sweet marzipan and date rolls were served, first to the nursing mother and then to the guests. Making marzipan was common enough in the Ottoman Middle East as well as in the Persian traditions that influenced Samarkandi cuisine. The proportions of almonds and sugar changed, and other ingredients like honey or rosewater were sometimes added, but Batya-Hannah insisted that the secret was in using fresh egg whites that rendered the sweetmeat particularly moist and nutritious. She would grind the peeled almonds until powdery, boil sugar syrup and pour it slowly into the almonds, adding egg whites until a smooth paste formed. In Jerusalem, she added to the marzipan tray her favourite childhood treat: date rolls. Jericho dates, a rarity in Samarkand, were commonly sold in the local market. The dough was made using butter, a common ingredient in Central Asia yet costly in Jerusalem, to show that no expense was spared to sustain the new mother. The rose-shaped rolls would melt in Zoulay's mouth as she nursed her newborn daughter.

## DATE ROLLS

Mix ¼ cup (60g) of soft butter, ½ cup (125ml) of olive oil, ½ cup (125ml) of water, 1 tablespoon of sugar and ½ teaspoon of salt. Add 3 cups (360g) of flour and mix until a dough is formed. Cover or wrap the dough and refrigerate it for 30 minutes. Preheat the oven to 180°C (gas mark 4). On a floured surface, roll the chilled dough into a 5mm-thick rectangular sheet (about 20x30cm). Spread on the dough 250g pure date paste, roll it up from the long edge into a log, and then cut the roll into 2cm-thick slices. Place the cookies on an oiled baking sheet and bake for 15–20 minutes, or until the dough is baked but still light in colour. Allow the cookies to cool before serving.

SAMARKANDI AND JERUSALEMITE CUISINES HAD MUCH IN common: pomegranates and chickpeas, coriander and lamb, rice and flatbread. But cooking them with local herbs and vegetables resulted in completely different flavours. There were chickpeas and fresh coriander in both cities, but in Jerusalem Zoulay might have eaten hummus with tahini, and tried zaatar and sumac. She could buy golden olive oil from a local press and dip a fresh warm pitta in it, or taste green olives marinated with slices of lemon and bay leaves. There were no peaches and apricots as there were in Samarkand, but there were grapefruit and zesty oranges. Zoulay started her daily routine by walking into the courtyard in the early-morning sun with her basket in hand, to gather fresh coriander and purple basil, red tomatoes and light green peppers, or figs and grapes in the late summer and beetroot and carrots in the winter. The distance between the garden and her kitchen was short, and perhaps suffocating at times, but living surrounded by greenery, among the sweet and fresh scents of fruit and leaves, was a blessing.

Zoulay's encounters with what Jerusalem so readily provided remain evident in the food she cooked, as I tasted it in the kitchen of my grandmother, her daughter Shulamit. She used much more lemon juice than she would have in Samarkand, where frosty winters made lemons a rarity until the 1950s, when Soviet scientists created the Tashkent lemon, a species that could resist the cold. Moving to the other side of Asia did not revolutionize her cooking but it did force her to adjust the delicate equilibrium of flavours in the dishes she had always made.

1. Yehezkel Mizrahi
as a young man,
c. 1905.

2. Yehezkel and
Joya (née Ben-Naim) Mizrahi,
1920s.

3. A view of Ludza, Latvia, in the 1920s.

*Above left* 4. Hananya and Zoulay Asheroff with their children, Tamara, Daniel, and Yehuda, in Moscow, 1926. Hananya's brothers, Yaakov and David, are standing behind.

*Above middle* 5. Gena-Rivka Adirim (née Kristal), 1927.

*Above right* 6. Esther Adirim (née Simanowitsch), 1928.

7. Zoulay Asheroff's USSR passport, 1927.

Пролетарии всех стран, соединяйтесь!

СОЮЗ СОВЕТСКИХ СОЦИАЛИСТИЧЕСКИХ РЕСПУБЛИК

ЗАГРАНИЧНЫЙ ПАСПОРТ.

Пред'явитель сего, граждан

и Союза Советских Социалистических Республик

отправляется за пределы С.С.С.Р.

в удостоверение чего и для свободного выезда, проживания за границей и обратного в'езда в С.С.С.Р. дан сей паспорт с приложением печати.

Настоящий паспорт действителен для проживания вне пределов С.С.С.Р. в течение со дня переезда границы.

Выдан 192 г.
в городе

СВЕДЕНИЯ О ПРЕДЪЯВИТЕЛЕ:

Время и место рождения 1893
Семейное положение

ПРИМЕТЫ:

Рост Глаза
Нос Волосы
Особые приметы —

Настоящий паспорт действителен для выезда из С.С.С.Р. до 192 г. через Контр.-Погран.-Пропускной Пункт

для возвращения обратно в С.С.С.Р. в течение срока действия паспорта через любой Контр.-Погран.-Пропускной Пункт.

№ 123833

Prolétaires de tous les pays, unissez-vous!

24/3 1927

№ 204

UNION

DES RÉPUBLIQUES SOVIÉTISTES SOCIALISTES.

PASSEPORT POUR L'ÉTRANGER.

Le porteur du présent

citoyen

et de l'Union des Républiques Soviétistes Socialistes

se rend au delà des frontières de l'U. R. S. S.

en foi de quoi et pour le libre départ, le séjour à l'étranger et pour le retour dans l'U.R.S.S. le présent passeport est délivré avec apposition du sceau.

Le présent passeport est valable pour le séjour hors des frontières de l'U.R.S.S. pour la durée de à partir du jour où la frontière a été franchie.

Délivré le 192
à

SIGNALEMENT DU PORTEUR:

Lieu et date de naissance 1893
État de famille

SIGNES:

Taille Yeux
Nez Cheveux
Signes particuliers —

8. A view of the central market of Riga, 1930s.

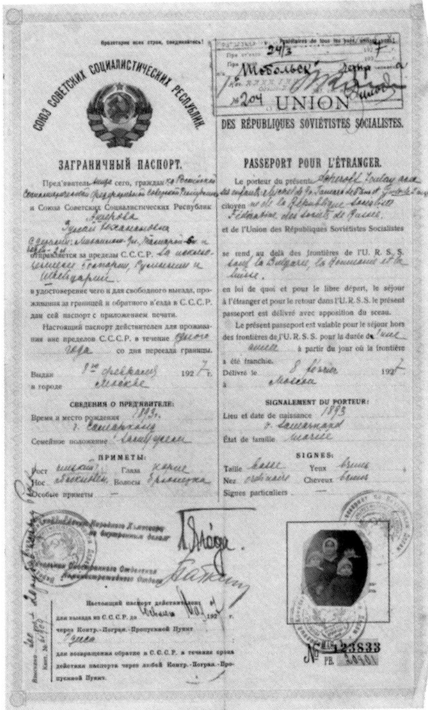

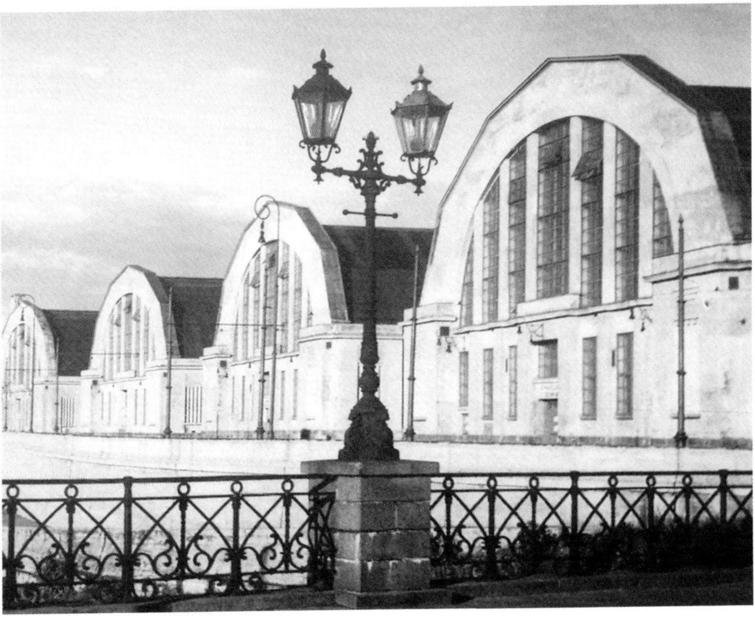

9. The Rosenboim family house near the market square of Trzibinia, 1931.

10. Hananya's siblings, Shlomo-Haim, Rachel and David Asheroff, with their families at the Asheroff house in Samarkand before emigrating to Jerusalem 1931.

11. Stabu Street, Riga, 1933.

12. Passport photos of Hirsch (Harry)
and Sara Adirim (née Goldschmit), 1934.

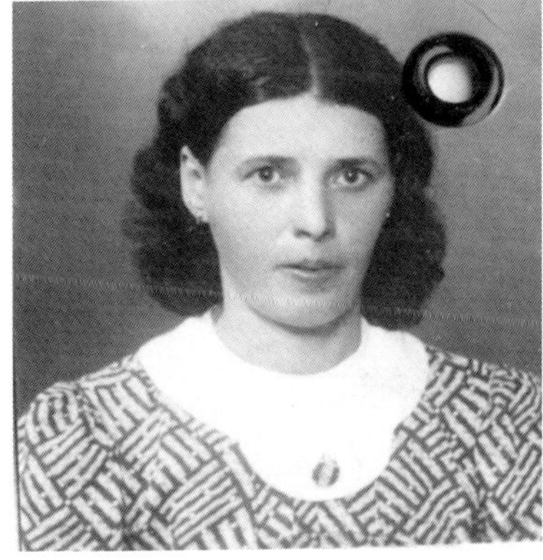

13. Passport photos of Selik
and Sara Adirim (née Katz), 1939.

*Above left*  14. Penina Asheroff (second left) and friends with cart, Jerusalem, early 1930s. *Above right*  15. Eliachar Mirzoeff visiting the Dome of the Rock, 1930s.

16. Esther Adirim and her grandchildren, Riga, c. 1937.

17. Taube Adirim (sitting in the bottom row, third from left)
with her group of Hashomer Hatzair, Riga, late 1930s.

18. Taube Adirim (right) with a friend in Riga, 1940.

19. Clara Khalfon and her son in Egypt, 1940s.

20. Yitzhak Mizrahi at eighteen.

21. Yitzhak Mizrahi, early 1940s.

# STUFFED COURGETTES

Take 10 small light green courgettes, cut off one end of each, extract their pulp (a melon spoon works well) and keep this to one side. Preheat the oven to 150°C (gas mark 2). Spread a large bunch of fresh mint on a baking sheet and bake it until it's dry. Separate the dry leaves from the stalks and crush the leaves to a coarse powder. Rinse 2 cups (400g) of basmati rice in cold water and then mix it with 350g of minced beef or lamb, ¼ cup (60ml) of olive oil, 2 cups (about 100g) of chopped coriander, and most of the dried mint (keep 2 tablespoons aside for the sauce). Fill the courgettes with the rice mixture, leaving some empty space for the rice to expand. If you have extra stuffing, you could put it in a cotton bag. In a large and wide ovenproof saucepan, cook the courgette pulp with ½ cup (125ml) of olive oil. Simmer for 15 minutes, then arrange the stuffed courgettes on top of the sauce and add the cotton bag if you have used it for the extra stuffing. Add another ½ cup (125ml) of olive oil, the juice of 2 lemons and the remaining mint, cover the pan with a lid and cook for 15 minutes over a medium heat. Remove the pan from the heat, add some water if the sauce seems too dry, and put it in the oven, with the lid on, to bake for 45 minutes, or until the courgettes are browned.

IN THE BUKHARAN STREETS IN THE LATE 1920S, ZOULAY led a secluded life in her family home. She seldom met people outside her immediate circle of friends and relatives, and had no interaction with the wider social and cultural milieus of Jerusalem. Similarly, the whole Bukharan neighbourhood seemed removed from city life. It was not geographically remote: only a forty-minute walk along Jaffa Street separates the Asheroff house from the Western Wall. Rather there were few roads in and out of the neighbourhood, even though modern transport, including motorcars, became more common in Jerusalem under the British Mandate. The residents of the neighbourhood – still exclusively Jewish – didn't embrace the spirit of religious and cultural diversity that characterized the historical city, nor did they succeed in realizing their utopian visions. They still saw Jerusalem as the ideal destination of religious pilgrimage and ignored its growing power in igniting nationalistic dreams. As the years went by, they became increasingly detached from daily chatter in the city's cafés, where people debated the rising tensions between the Jewish and Arab populations, and their British governors. With few connections in the newly established networks of Zionist institutions, the Bukharan community seemed to have misinterpreted Jerusalem's past and future alike.

Some of the neighbourhood's inhabitants, however, found ways into the heart of Jerusalem's present. Zoulay's young sister-in-law, Penina, discovered in the city an exciting change from her native Samarkand. Penina was an unusual figure in the Asheroff family; she was the only woman who didn't cook. The youngest daughter of Zion and Batya-Hannah, she grew up almost as an only child because her older brothers and sisters already had families of their own. In Jerusalem, Penina turned into the free-minded and opinionated woman that Zoulay could never have been. She was fierce and independent, disregarding the social conventions that tied Zoulay to her family and home, and lived on her own terms.

Penina's youth in Jerusalem is much better documented than the lives of the rest of her family. Her grandchildren sent me a stream of photos from the early 1930s, showing her as a young woman, perhaps twenty or a little older. In one, she is sitting on a mule wearing a short skirt and a woollen jumper. In another she sports a floral dress and sits on a cart with three friends, a straw hat at her feet. In a blurry image she is laughing among a group of girls in elegant frocks, standing in front of houses under construction, perhaps in one of Jerusalem's new neighbourhoods; elsewhere she is posing, hat in hand, on a pile of stones in a vast open field.

In all of these pictures, Penina stares straight at the camera in a way that Zoulay never did. She is fully aware of, and apparently feels entitled to, being documented. In a group of young people, she stands in a graceful pose that shows off her high-heeled shoes and her embroidered silk dress, tightened at the waist with a belt. The same dress makes repeated appearances: at the seaside, by the river, next to a modern car, at the new British War Cemetery in Mount Scopus. Penina might not have an extensive wardrobe, but she was out and about, exploring the land, its nature and its archaeology, travelling unchaperoned with her friends. Her explorations are documented at least in images, if not in her own words. She is never in the kitchen, not even remotely so.

Penina's emancipation surprises me because no other woman in the family was given a similar opportunity. The Ottomans left, the British arrived, yet the traditional ways of the Bukharan community remained largely unchanged. At family gatherings,

Hananya still expected to preside over glorious feasts with a succession of dishes, from palao to sirkaniz, stuffed chicken and roast mutton, black tea and arak. Zoulay would still be the one who cooked them, later assisted by her daughters Tamara and Shulamit. Penina did not join them in the kitchen, seemingly not obliged to do so. And if she was, she didn't seem to care. Perhaps, with her friends, she would venture out to eat, defying the usual codes of behaviour for Samarkandi women, who would never eat in restaurants. She might have sipped afternoon tea at the luxurious King David Hotel, which opened in 1931 and immediately became a magnet for British officers and Jerusalem's high society.

Penina figured out better than most of the family how to live well in Jerusalem, which was changing quickly, testing the Asheroffs' attempts to integrate. Transformed by waves of Jewish immigration from Eastern Europe and British construction projects, Jerusalem was no longer the Levantine city of Batya-Hannah's youth, where Jewish and Arab merchants worked together in the market stalls. The division of the city into four 'quarters', each associated with a religious community, must have seemed alien to sixty-year-old Zion, who had grown up embracing Jerusalem's multiplicity and diversity.[5] Its British rulers sought to give the city order, to parcel and define it, and by doing so they accentuated the religious and ethnic divides.

The position of the Bukharan Quarter, bordering the fields at the outskirts of the urban area, made it vulnerable to attacks. As the line of demarcation between the Jewish and Arab communities became increasingly evident, violence erupted. Like all the young people in her social milieu, Penina joined the Jewish armed militia, the Haganah. This organization was founded in the early

1920s to defend the Jewish population in Palestine from Arab attacks. After the Arab riots of 1929, when the Haganah helped protect Jewish communities, it gained greater influence and its membership grew significantly. During the subsequent decade, the organization's structure transformed into a more centralized army. The British, who adopted an imperial policy in favour of local self-defence military organizations, initially granted their support and provided armaments and training.[6]

Membership in the Haganah was open to women, who could also take active roles in combat. Years later Penina said that she would have been ashamed to stay out of the action. She discovered that she was a good shot and soon became the commander of a group of ten young women who met at night. Although the Haganah meetings were legal, in her later recollections Penina remembered a sense of clandestine secrecy: members had to give a password at the door to be granted entry. She did not know the other members personally; all they had in common was their Jewishness and shared belief in the cause of Zionism.

Penina always insisted that she had felt very content with her life in Jerusalem. She didn't seem to share her brother Hananya's disappointment with the conservative power-seeking leaders of the Bukharan community who allowed the neighbourhood's decline. She didn't seem concerned by the lack of cultural and healthcare services, or by the discrimination against women in the neighbourhood's administration. She simply turned away from the neighbourhood and embraced all that the city had to offer, including going to the cinema in the city centre.

It was at the cinema that she met Eliachar Mirzoeff, a wealthy fur trader whose merchant family was originally from Bukhara. In the early twentieth century, different branches of his family left

Bukhara and settled in London and New York. He invited her to see a movie, and bought tickets for the best seats in the house. Penina, who shunned the modest lifestyle of her sister-in-law and her nieces, taking her lead from her brother's high social standards, was delighted. When she introduced him to her father and brothers, their marriage was already a done deal. Penina may have been perfectly happy in Jerusalem, but she was ready for the next adventure. Perhaps it was the confidence of feeling at home in the world that made her emigrate again. She also knew that her husband would be able to give her a life of comfort and pleasure in their chosen new homeland, Britain. The marriage would make her a respectable British lady, Mrs Mirzoeff, forever admired by the rest of her family, who would come to visit her comfortable house in north London.

It was in this identity that I encountered Penina as a cook. In the pages of Claudia Roden's classic *Book of Jewish Food*, Penina Mirzoeff provided the recipes for the food of the Jews of Bukhara and Samarkand.[7] Then in her sixties, she described how to make osh-sevo in the oven, and how to prepare khalti-bakhsh using a linen bag, a method that Roden describes as specifically Jewish.[8] At first glance, I did not associate Mrs Mirzeoff with my mythical aunt Penina, who, according to family stories, had conquered London with her charm and wit. Penina's family history, whether in Samarkand or Jerusalem, was not mentioned. In London, she cooked the recipes of the Mirzeoff family. Even with her children and grandchildren, she discussed at length the dishes served at the table of her husband's family dinners, not those of her mother. It is ironic that Penina, who had so fiercely resisted her own family kitchen, should have become an emblem of Samarkandi cuisine in London. But from the descriptions of her family's Bukharan food, I was able to piece together Zoulay's lost recipe for khalti-sevo, a special version of osh-sevo cooked not in a pot but in a linen bag immersed in broth and baked overnight.

# KHALTI-SEVO

**(inspired by Penina Mirzoeff's recipe in
Claudia Roden's *Book of Jewish Food*)**

Core, remove the seeds, and chop 1 sour apple and 1 quince (no need to peel the fruit). In a large bowl, mix 1½ cups (300g) of washed basmati rice, the chopped apple and quince, a handful of dark seedless grapes and a handful each of raisins and chopped dates. Add salt to taste and put the mixture in a linen bag, so that the bag is three-quarters full. Tie the bag firmly and place it in an ovenproof pot a little bigger than the bag. Cover the bag with hot beef stock (about 1.5 litres), and add 1 apple and 1 quince, both cut into quarters, and a handful of raisins. Preheat the oven to 120°C (gas mark ½). Bring the pot to a boil on the stove, then cover it with a lid and put it in the oven to cook slowly for 6–8 hours, or until the rice is cooked and the sauce is dense and purple. To serve, remove the rice from the sack, place in a large plate, and top with a generous spoonful of the sauce.

BY THE TIME PENINA RELOCATED TO LONDON, HANANYA was also feeling the urge to move again. The stifling air of the Bukharan Quarter, which continued to resist his reformist visions of progress, pushed him towards the countryside. He spotted a good business opportunity in the expanding agricultural settlements in the fertile plains of Palestine. In 1934, Zoulay once again packed her beautiful embroideries and gold-rimmed blue teacups, and the family set off to their new home in the small town of Petah Tikva.

**_Chapter 5_**

# ZOULAY ASHEROFF IN PETAH TIKVA, 1934–1942

IN 1934, HANANYA, ZOULAY AND THEIR CHILDREN FINALLY settled down in a place of their own. After living in the Asheroff family houses in Samarkand and Jerusalem, it was the first time they had to find a house for themselves. Without much ado, Hananya rented a small white villa with a red-tiled roof facing an olive grove in the centre of Petah Tikva. Its architecture was unassuming: just a simple building with running water, electricity and a modern kitchen with an ice box and a gas oven. It had a porch at the front and a patch of land at the back.

Petah Tikva was one of the first Jewish settlements in Palestine. In the late nineteenth century, its founders bought from a wealthy Jaffa merchant some land near the village of Umm Labeis or Mulabbis (a name which means 'sugared almonds', testifying to the history of almond-growing there). The settlers called their village 'a door of hope', inspired by a biblical verse about a fertile valley: 'I will give her vineyards from there, And the Valley of Achor as a door of hope; She shall sing there, As in the days of her youth, As in the day when she came up from the land of Egypt' (Hosea 2:15). The land they bought was in the midst of malaria-infested swamps long considered inhospitable, and the settlers' decades-long efforts to drain the swamps and cultivate the land supplied material for Zionist myths of the kind that I was taught at school. By the 1930s it had been transformed into an agricultural town – the swamps had dried up – and was a place that offered the Asheroffs a fresh start, in the heart of Zionist Palestine.

Hananya was attracted to the newness of Petah Tikva, oriented towards the future, without the centuries-long history that had shaped, and at times burdened, Jerusalem. Maybe it reminded him of Samarkand's rural communities, where people lived so close to nature. Yet in Petah Tikva everything had to be made anew. The Jewish settlers wanted to show that, with their modern knowhow, they were able to do what the previous Arab inhabitants supposedly could not achieve, namely to change the swampy land into a thriving town sustained by its agricultural industry. They were determined to find new ways to tame nature and transform it to their advantage.[1]

I grew up in Tel Aviv, only a few kilometres away, but I don't remember ever visiting Petah Tikva. When I began to write this book, I decided to remedy this and follow in Zoulay and Hananya's footsteps. Leaving the highway, I had to navigate my way around blocks of nondescript high-rises, then past the large hospital where, thirty-odd years ago, I was born. 'Place of birth: Petah Tikva' is printed on all my official documents like a constant reminder. A reminder of what? I never felt any connection to my grey, unappealing native city, whose agricultural past is now covered by a veil of asphalt and cement. Driving through it didn't change my initial instincts. Maybe now, with Zoulay and Hananya, I would see it with fresh eyes.

My first stop was the municipal archive, housed in a small building near the local museums of art and municipal history. I hoped to find some evidence of my ancestors' lives here, although I was not sure what I was looking for. The archivist directed me to the deeds for Hananya's house and plantations, his almond groves and orange orchards, which are now large residential suburbs.[2]

Hananya bought orange and almond plantations because he planned to enter the prosperous business of exporting fruit to Europe.[3] Petah Tikva was, at the time, surrounded by expansive orange orchards. The Hebrew name for the fruit of the orange tree was only coined in the early twentieth century, as Biblical Hebrew did not have one. There was a word for orchard, *pardes*, which shares a common etymological Persian root with the English 'paradise'. Maybe inspired by Western images of the paradisal apple, they called the orange *tapuah zahav*, or golden apple. The reference to gold seemed to allude not only to the colour but also to a shared hope that the plantations would generate an abundance of wealth.

Ironically, Petah Tikva's rural appeal led to its urbanization. In the 1930s, the settlement absorbed thousands of immigrants from Eastern Europe, Bulgaria, Bukhara and Samarkand, like the Asheroffs and many of their relatives. They were attracted to Petah Tikva's agricultural success and were all treated with suspicion by the original Jewish settlers and their families.[4] Despite Hananya's indefatigable optimism, being an immigrant in Petah Tikva was not easy. While he could claim family roots in Jerusalem, making him less of a stranger, here in Petah Tikva he was a foreigner, a newcomer who had to do his best to belong.

Petah Tikva was a small, conservative place. Every unfamiliar habit, unusual style of dress or foreign food were frowned upon or ridiculed. Hananya sought the good opinion of his neighbours by engaging in public life. The archives told me that he was well known in town. As a property owner he had the right to vote and to be voted onto the local council. Two years after his arrival, he was elected as the farmers' representative on the municipal council and put in charge of healthcare.[5] Before the hospital was built on the outskirts of town – the one I was eventually born in – he coordinated medical treatment for the city's residents in Tel Aviv, at the council's expense. His socialist and progressive ideas that had been rejected by his fellow Bukharans in Jerusalem finally found a welcoming home.

While Hananya strived to climb the political ladder, Zoulay was yet to feel at home in her new house. In the backyard, Hananya built her a summer kitchen where she would wash and clean her vegetables, chopping and preparing them for cooking in a large metal pot set on coals. He built a small tandoor, where she could bake noni-tokhi and goshgidja pastries. He added a small wooden shed that served as a cool pantry for dairy and meat, where the milkman left his bottles every morning. Inside the house she also had a Samarkandi 'winter kitchen', with a modern kerosene primus cooker instead of a traditional hearth, though she still preferred using the tandoor oven outside.

She found it more difficult to blend into the local community than her husband. Wearing colourful silk frocks even when she went to pick up her daughter from school, she could not escape the disapproving gaze of her neighbours. In her summer kitchen, she cooked curious dishes where everyone could see them. One of her favourite, goat's intestines filled with spleen and other offal, was a special delicacy. The ingredients were considered inexpensive in the 1930s – though nowadays not easily available – but required long, careful preparation, and skills beyond the reach of many cooks. Zoulay soaked the intestines in water for hours to clean them. Then, she stuffed them with the offal and steamed them over hot water. The result was a scented, full-flavoured sausage that was served as the centre of the Passover eve dinner. This dish was certainly not a common one in Petah Tivka's homes and restaurants. Eating stuffed goat's guts was a clear mark of otherness.

Yet, cooking outdoors in the garden, as she had always done in Samarkand and then Jerusalem, must have been particularly pleasing. The garden changed with every season, and so did her cooking. By the outdoor kitchen, she planted a vegetable garden, which was soon full of courgettes and tomatoes, coriander and mint, radish, beets, carrots and the special purple basil that Hananya used to freshen up his garlicky tomato salad. By the pillars of the large porch, where the family dined on summer nights, Hananya planted a cutting of the vine that he had brought from Samarkand. Eventually, it clambered above the porch, bearing plump clusters of sweet grapes that hung over the dining table, just as they had in Samarkand. It was a comfortingly familiar sight in a garden full of Mediterranean plants that must have been new to Zoulay: orange, clementine, bergamot and mandarin trees, as well as huge sour red Surinam cherry trees and purple passion-fruit, with its delicate flowers that turned into round fruit full of fragrant juice. I can imagine her standing in the kitchen, breathing in the sweet blossom of oranges and almonds that found its way in from the garden.

Not all her culinary choices were dictated by taste or climate, though. In the city's archive, I discovered that the butchers in Petah Tikva did not sell lamb. A group of Bukharan immigrants petitioned the council for a licence to open their own slaughter-house, to provide fresh mutton, 'which was necessary for our sick women, by doctor's orders'.[6] The council's reply is not recorded, but the way in which my family's favourite dishes changed suggests that the petition was rejected. Zoulay started to substitute mutton fat with olive oil in her osh-palao and oshi-bakhsh dishes. She replaced her fragrant lamb's broth with a rich chicken soup, decorated with golden dots of fat. Instead of stuffed lamb, she filled chickens with rice and coriander, and roasted them until crisp and brown. Scarcity was an opportunity to invent, to extend her cooking beyond the traditions, to express her own creativity.

# MEDITERRANEAN PALAO

Soak 2 cups (400g) of basmati rice in hot water for 30 minutes. Soak 1 cup (150g) of peeled almonds and 1 cup (150g) of light raisins in hot water for 30 minutes. Heat 3 tablespoons of olive oil in a large pan, and add 3 chicken thighs. Cook them until the meat is golden and sealed on all sides, and then remove them from the pot. Using the same pan, now put in 2 finely chopped onions and sauté them on a low heat until they are just turning gold. While the onions are cooking, peel 6 large carrots and cut them into thin strips. Place the chicken thighs back in the pan, on top of the cooked onions, and cover them with the carrots, adding 1 teaspoon of salt. Drain the rice, almonds and raisins and add them to the pan. Do not stir. Add ½ teaspoon of salt, ¼ cup (60ml) of olive oil, and enough water to cover the rice. Bring the pan to a boil, then cover it with a clean tea towel and a lid, and cook on a low heat for 15–20 minutes, or until the rice is cooked.

IN THE WINTER, THE HOUSE WAS FULL OF ORANGES, LARGE and juicy, stored in wooden crates under the beds. Zoulay made candied peel by boiling long strips of orange rind in water until they lost their bitter taste, and then cooking them in a sugary syrup that preserved their colour and zing. New ingredients encouraged her to try out new recipes, too. Cakes were completely absent from traditional Samarkandi cuisine, but in Petah Tikva she baked one for the first time. She squeezed the sweet and refreshing juice of ripe clementines and added it to eggs whisked with sugar, folded in some white flour, then poured the batter into an aluminium tin to bake in her new gas oven. The result was a light and airy cake that she served in thick slices on Saturday afternoons.

## CLEMENTINE CAKE

Preheat the oven to 180°C (gas mark 4). Beat 5 egg whites with ½ cup (125g) of sugar until stiff peaks form. In a separate bowl, mix together 5 egg yolks, ½ cup (125ml) of olive oil, the juice of 5 or 6 clementines (or small mandarins or oranges) and ½ a lemon, and the zest of 1 clementine. In another bowl, sift 2 cups (250g) of plain flour and 2 teaspoons (10g) of baking powder. Using a spatula, gently fold the egg whites into the egg yolk mixture, and gradually add the flour mixture until it all looks uniform. Pour the cake mixture into a well-greased 22cm baking tin and bake in the preheated oven for 45 minutes, or until the cake is golden and firm to touch. Let it cool before turning onto a plate and serving.

HANANYA STARTED TO EXPERIMENT WITH GRAFTING: HE cut a sliver with a bud from a clementine tree, then inserted it into an incision in an orange tree, taped it, let it sit and heal all winter, then pruned it again. The following year, he did the same with a sliver of tangerine. Within a few years, oranges, clementines and tangerines magically appeared on the tree's branches, to the great pride of its owner. His bergamot tree received a very special treatment: when each fruit was emerging from its white flower, Hananya trapped it in a glass bottle. The fruit continued to grow inside the bottles that clinked in the afternoon wind. After the fruit were ripe, Hananya carefully cut them and their bottles from the tree, then topped up the bottles with home-made arak, which absorbed the fruit's delicate bittersweet fragrance.

In an interview he gave to the Hebrew University in his later years, Hananya said that he travelled by mule every day from his home to the orchard.[7] In fact, after a short stint as a farmer he handed the majority of the physical chores to expert Arab workers and got himself a job at the local branch of the Anglo-Palestine Bank, which provided most of the funding for local farmers and fruit merchants. His office was located in a respectable yellow villa on Montefiore Street, just behind the market, in the heart of Petah Tikva. Despite the prestigious position given to farming in Zionist ideology, a desk job in finance was more in line with Hananya's aspirations and personal style.

Many Bukharan migrants moved to Petah Tikva. Some, like Hananya and Zoulay, moved there from a previous residence in Palestine, and others, like some of their brothers and sisters, arrived directly from Samarkand.[8] In the new social landscape of Petah Tikva, they were no longer religious pilgrims or international merchants, but a diasporic community of migrants. While some might have arrived there out of choice, others had certainly been forced to flee Soviet persecution in Central Asia, through the dangerous desert pass in Mashad in north-east Iran, not far from the Caspian Sea. The routes they took and the motivation behind their displacement were different from those of their ancestors, who travelled frequently to the Bukharan Quarter of Jerusalem. The transition was hardly surprising in a world increasingly shaped by aggressive nationalism. Moving from country to country, whether for trade or for religion, was increasingly frowned upon; people were supposed to have a national home and stay there.

Hananya, as we have seen, was quick to find his way into the local community. He loved being surrounded by people, giving them his opinions and making his voice heard. He enjoyed passing his evenings at Café Atara on the main street, or later at the Blue Bird Café, where the local 'high society' and British officers danced and listened to live music, drank gin and tonic or Cinzano vermouth and played cards.[9] Hananya would sit on the elegant terrace and sip his arak, charming anyone who would listen with his tales. He felt at ease among the local crowd of Zionist reformers, socialists and farmers, bankers and industrialists: he had a story for everyone's taste. Now a middle-aged man, he was finally given the respect and recognition he desired.

In Petah Tikva, women were able to study and work, and, obviously, to shop and sell goods in the market. Women would promenade in the city's unpaved streets in the afternoon, or sit with their children at the kiosk in the park for a treat of ice cream and soda. But as far as I can tell, Zoulay stayed close to home. Nothing prevented her from going out and about, from making friends and enjoying an autonomous life. If she didn't do any of that, maybe she simply didn't want to. She did, however, go food shopping. In 1930, Petah Tikva built a new, covered market with permanent stalls and electric lighting. In the city archive, I found the original plans elegantly drawn on brown paper by a local architect: it was beautifully designed and had areas allocated for fruit, household goods, beauty and general stores.[10] It was perhaps less exciting than Samarkand's famous bazaar, yet it was a modern and well-stocked market, with stalls laden with fresh produce, jute bags of lentils and flour, bread and cakes, and even live cattle and chickens. The competition between the vendors was fierce, commerce was thriving, and some shops even remained open until eleven at night, to give the farmers time to buy groceries or run errands after their working day in the orchards.

The market attracted merchants and customers from all over the region, both Jewish and Arab. Away from the sheltered Bukharan Quarter, in Petah Tikva Zoulay could encounter the people who inhabited the land she lived in. Even at a time of increasing tensions between Arab and Jewish communities, which the British rulers failed to alleviate, the market remained a friendly and welcoming space. Every morning, Arab merchants arrived on mules laden with fresh vegetables from their fields. Their presence was not uncontested by the town's shop owners, whose resentment was not really born of nationalism; rather, they begrudged the apparent trade advantage of the Arabs who could offer lower prices because they did not rent a stall or pay municipal taxes. Despite these complaints, the Arab farmers continued to come to the market and the pragmatic residents of Petah Tikva continued to buy their produce.

On her return from the market, Zoulay would ask Shulamit and Avner, the youngest children, to help inspect the chickpeas and the rice. She taught them how to look for blemishes, little stones and, worst of all, worms or flies. Their tiny nimble fingers would pass the good grains of rice from one side of the tray to another. In the winter, they would then sit in the small, warm kitchen and make rice balls together. For the children, it was a game, a simple thing that could be prepared playfully, without the careful attention that Zoulay gave to other dishes. Shulamit was soon expert at rolling round balls of cooked rice, mixed with egg and filled with meat and herbs, that Zoulay then baked in the oven until crisp.

## RICE BALLS

Preheat the oven to 180°C (gas mark 4). Put 2 cups (400g) of washed rice in a saucepan, add 3 cups of water (or enough to cover the rice by 2cm) and 1 teaspoon of salt. Bring to the boil over a high heat and simmer for 5 minutes. Lower the heat and cover the pot with a lid. Steam the rice for about 10 minutes, until the rice is cooked and slightly sticky. Set it aside to cool down. In the meantime, heat 2 tablespoons (30ml) of olive oil in a pan and saute 1 finely chopped medium-sized onion until it is golden. Add 150g of minced beef and cook it for a minute or two. Remove the mince and onions from the pan. Add 20g of chopped parsley to the meat and season it with salt and pepper. When the rice has cooled down, mix into it 2 beaten eggs and 4 tablespoons (35g) of flour. Flatten a little of the rice mixture in the palm of your hand and fill it with some of the meat mixture. Add more rice on top and close it to form a ball about the size of a small apple. Repeat the process with the remainder of the rice and meat. Place the rice balls on an oiled baking sheet and sprinkle them with a little olive oil. Put the baking sheet in the preheated oven and bake for 30 minutes or until golden. Serve hot.

SHULAMIT AND AVNER WERE GROWING UP WITH A SENSE of liberty that Zoulay could not have imagined at their age. From a young age they were out and about, exploring. Their brothers and sister were old enough to ignore these younger, mischievous siblings. And so the two passed their afternoons running around the orange orchards, their magical place. They loved the scent of the sweet Shamouti oranges, but also enjoyed wandering around the packaging plant, where each fruit was carefully wrapped with colourful printed tissue paper and placed in a wooden crate, awaiting shipment to Europe. In the winter, the whole family would be enlisted to help with the wrapping and packaging, before the oranges began to rot. The younger children soon got tired of working, and instead sat on a high tree branch and watched the workers while sucking the sweet flesh of the ripe oranges.

On hot days, Shulamit and Avner would swim in the irrigation tanks that served to water the trees. In the quiet calm of the orchard, these large pools were irresistible. Diving into their cool water was a secret pleasure, obviously more pleasing because it was severely prohibited. Avner climbed up the ladder and jumped in, followed by his more cautious older sister. The limpid water cooled their tanned skin and the orange trees filtered the bright sunlight, while shifting in the warm breeze.

One day, as they were swimming in circles in the deep pool, a loud sucking noise hinted that the irrigation system had been switched on, draining the pools into the tubes that watered the trees. The water level began to lower and the children could no longer reach the rim and climb out. They shouted for help, splashing and banging on the tank noisily, but the orchards were empty. It was a hot summer afternoon, and all the workers had left. Despite this, only one question bothered their anxious minds: what would their father say if they did not show up on time for dinner? Just as they began to feel exhausted from screaming, a face appeared at the top of the tank; it was a young man who worked in the orchard and lived in one of the Arab villages on the outskirts of town. He lowered a ladder, climbed down and fished them out. They were home in time for dinner and Hananya never knew.

After sunset, the Asheroff house woke up. People swarmed in

and out, with no need for an invitation. Without a fridge or freezer, Zoulay had to cook fresh meals every day. There were always salads: fresh tomatoes seasoned with garlic the way Hananya liked, and another with tomatoes, cucumbers and onions, with plenty of parsley on top. On the table, there were always baskets of crispy noni-tokhi and soft and warm round bread sprinkled with nigella seeds that Zoulay baked outside in the tandoor. She always made plenty of food, never knowing exactly how many people would turn up for dinner. Her eldest children, Daniel and Misha, worked in Jerusalem but often came to eat with the family. If her brothers Gabriel and Raphael came with their families, she would take out of the oven their favourite paper-thin layered pastries with meat and herbs, or a large pot of stuffed artichokes in lemon juice. Hananya's brother Yaakov would come on horse and cart from Tel Aviv, with his wife Yafa, their three children and a large tray of her speciality, home-made bichak, a delicious sweetish pumpkin-filled pastry.

## BICHAK

Finely chop 1 medium-sized onion and fry it in 3 tablespoons (45ml) of olive oil. Add 1 teaspoon of sugar. When the onion is golden, add about 500g of peeled and grated butternut squash or pumpkin (as an alternative to grating the pumpkin, you can also steam it and then mush with a fork). Stir-fry the onion and pumpkin over a high heat and season it with salt, pepper and sugar to taste. Continue frying, as the pumpkin will reduce its volume by half, until there is no more liquid in the pan. Remove the mixture from the pan and leave it to cool. Make a dough using 2¼ cups (300g) of plain flour, ½ cup (125ml) of oil, 20g fresh yeast, 1 teaspoon of salt, 1 teaspoon of sugar, and as much warm water as necessary to make a firm dough (usually about 250ml). Knead the dough well, cover it with a towel and leave it to rise for an hour. When it has risen, roll the dough until it's about 5mm thick, then cut it out into circles using a cup. Preheat the oven to 200°C (gas mark 6). In the centre of each circle, place 1 teaspoon of the pumpkin filling, and then fold the sides of the dough over the filling to form a triangle and pinch the seams together to close the pastry. Place the pastries on an oiled baking sheet with the seams facing down, brush each one with egg yolk (you can sprinkle some sesame or nigella seeds on top) and bake them in the oven until they are golden brown.

AFTER MY INITIAL TOUR OF THE ARCHIVES, I RETURNED TO Petah Tikva once more, this time accompanied by my grandmother Shulamit. I was surprised to discover that, despite living close by in Tel Aviv, she had never returned to the city where she grew up. Perhaps it had changed too much, and going back no longer seemed to make sense. But some places from her childhood were still there: we walked past the elementary school she attended, to the street where the family house used to stand (the house itself had been replaced by a smallish apartment block). The olive grove that she remembered standing across the road was now a playground with a slide and a swing. Shulamit was thrilled to discover that the Anglo-Palestine Bank offices, where her father used to work, still existed. The villa had been beautifully renovated and rebranded as a new social centre for women. The market remained, too, but she hardly recognized it. The Petah Tikva of her youth was a whole new city, made of concrete high-rises, roundabouts and shopping malls. The scent of oranges and almonds lived only in her memory.

Less than a month after Shulamit's tenth birthday, in 1939, the world entered another global conflict. The Second World War scrambled Hananya's carefully made plans. Maritime embargoes stopped all exports from Palestine, leaving his oranges to rot in the warehouse. Petah Tikva, which relied on its orchards, struggled to survive. Under instructions from the British governor, the mayor started to ration food, providing the residents with stamps for vital products such as sugar, milk and bread.[11] When her weekly allowance of sugar was gone, Zoulay used last summer's fruit preserves to sweeten her tea.

When Hananya's parents, Zion and Batya-Hannah, moved to Petah Tikva in 1938, they had opened a small grocery shop in the city centre. Zion's health was deteriorating. He became weaker and started to lose his hearing, but nonetheless had no intention of resting at home. In his old age, he lived a humble life, after losing much of his wealth in his attempts to provide passports, visas and travel permits for seven of his children and their families to emigrate from Samarkand to Jerusalem. One day, a young girl entered his shop and bought a cone of crystal sugar. Shortly afterwards she returned with some British policemen, who accused Zion of selling rationed food at exorbitant prices. His sons bailed him from prison, but Zion soon realized that he was unable to adapt to this new place, with its new laws, under the auspices of a new empire. He retired to his home, to his Bible studies and to his beloved wife, observing life in Petah Tikva as a curious foreigner, an eternal stranger.

The war swept Palestine into an age of even greater instability. Local conflicts were exacerbated by global alliances. Tel Aviv was bombed in an Italian air raid, and there were even fears of a Nazi invasion.[12] Once again, Hananya was forced to make plans to keep his family safe. The orchards were no longer a reliable source of income, and he lost his seemingly unshakeable faith in their long-term return. Following a friend's advice, he exchanged them for a small semi-detached house in a working-class neighbourhood in southern Tel Aviv.

With the benefit of hindsight, the family would look on this decision as the most unfortunate he'd ever made. Sometimes, my grandmother would say, it is better to stay put and wait the crisis out: in the subsequent decades the orchards could have been sold to real-estate developers for a fortune. But in the middle of a world war, Hananya wanted security and comfort, despite having to start over, yet again, this time in his mid-fifties. And so, in 1942, he and Zoulay packed up their home again. Along with their youngest children, Shulamit and Avner, and Hananya's elderly parents Zion and Batya-Hannah, they moved, for the last time, to the house in Tel Aviv.

*Chapter 6*

# A MEDITERRANEAN INTERLUDE

JOYA BEN-NAIM WAS A BEAUTIFUL YOUNG WOMAN: HER dark eyes stare out from one of the only photographs of her that I have. Fashionably dressed in a 1920s flapper dress, she looks sad, or perhaps distracted. She was married off to a much older man, a rich merchant recently settled in Jerusalem who promised her a comfortable and leisurely life. His name was Yehezkel Mizrahi. Their eldest son, Yitzhak, was my maternal grandfather.

Yitzhak didn't like to talk about his family, and I know little about their history. Their full names, places of origin, dates of birth and death, were all shrouded in mystery. When his mother died in 1962, Yitzhak wrote on her tombstone the name Margalit Efrati. Much later, I discovered that this was a name she had assumed late in life, a name he had made up for her. Against the Jewish tradition, he did not write the names of her parents on her tomb, nor her date of birth. Perhaps he felt that by eliminating details that he considered inconvenient, he could invent a new family history, one more in line with the zeitgeist.

Why was Grandfather Yitzhak so keen to turn away from his past? What was he trying to eliminate so forcefully? The silence made me curious, but my inquisitiveness was not enough to make Yitzhak open up. He had a roundabout way of answering my questions, leading me far away from concrete dates and places, towards the more suggestive and abstract realm of memories, sharing only those moments from his early years that he deemed worthy of remembrance. While his family history remained largely hidden from us, he was proud of his days as a soldier, telling us stories of how he had fought to establish and defend the state of Israel. Only years later, after he had died, did I understand that perhaps the two issues were closely linked.

Despite Yitzhak's intentional vagueness, over the years I've pieced together shreds of information to create a picture of his – and his family's – past. It was a moving image, reflecting the lives of people who chose displacement as their mode of living. There were episodes of home-building in Haifa, Algeria, Aleppo, Alexandria, Jerusalem and Marseilles, but the fact remains that Joya, Yehezkel and their forebears were Mediterranean people whose families travelled back and forth across the sea.

As I tried to make sense of my ancestors' frequent moves, the lives of the family's women remained as nebulous as ever. Wives and daughters were rarely mentioned in official documents, in formal census records, or in newspaper articles. Even when they do appear, they sometimes remain nameless, only noted as a wife, a daughter, a mother. Tracking down the histories of these women turned out to be challenging not only for lack of historical sources, but also because a matrilineal family history is necessarily complicated by name changes. In every generation, women took their husband's last name, and their original birth name disappeared without a trace. It was by pure chance that a distant relative told me that Joya's maiden name was Ben-Naim. After her marriage, it was never mentioned again.

Joya and her sister Clara were born in Haifa: Clara in 1890, and Joya in 1899. Their parents had moved to Haifa after they were married, from the smaller town of Tiberias. In this period, Tiberias – just a few thousand residents at the best of times – saw a great hustle and bustle of visitors.[1] Some arrived looking for a religious revelation at the biblical lakeside or by a rabbi's tomb. Others wanted to bring progress – in the form of the Christian faith, Western medicine or free education – to the local inhabitants. A small gathering of houses nestled between palm trees against the glimmering water, Tiberias seemed dormant, but in fact it was in constant flux. In the archives I discovered that many Jewish migrants from North Africa ended up there, including a Ben-Naim family from Tétouan, a major Mediterranean port city in northern Morocco.[2] Could this have been Joya's family? As the women of the family were not mentioned in the records, it is hard to tell.

It is almost certain, however, that the Ben-Naim family had roots in North Africa. Joya spoke French but not Ladino, the typical language of the Sephardi Jews of Ottoman Palestine. She also had French travel documents, a possible clue to her family's past in the French Empire. If not from Morocco, her family might have come from Algeria. Like many Jewish families, they could have left Algeria after the French invasion of 1830, when rivalries between the European empires destabilized the region. The Ben-Naims would have been one of dozens of Jewish families who travelled to Palestine from the port of Oran hoping for new trading opportunities. While most settled in Jerusalem or Jaffa, some were attracted to the smaller, cosmopolitan towns of the north, where

Arabs, Christians and Jews of all origins lived together alongside missionaries, pilgrims and tourists. By the end of the nineteenth century, Tiberias had more than two thousand Jewish residents, making up the majority of its multinational and multi-religious population. The Ottoman governors invested in new rail services and thermal baths, which made it an appealing destination for travellers from the wider region and beyond.[3]

When my archival research generated little insight into Joya's past, I retreated into the kitchen. There, I could still feel the echoes of her family's Mediterranean crossings. In the food that she used to make – simple recipes that I learned from my grandfather in Tel Aviv – there were untold hints of the cosmopolitan life led by her family of merchants. I've reproduced Joya's thick bean and tomato soup served with a white mound of fresh rice, I've stuffed peppers and cooked them in tomato sauce, I have fried chopped onions for her lentil mejadra and cooked golden-brown sofrito with peppered meatballs and cinnamon-covered potatoes. These were dishes of people who lived close to their Arab and Muslim neighbours, of people who inhabited the southern Mediterranean without looking north to Europe for guidance or inspiration. Despite Joya's fluency in French, there was little of France on her dinner table. Judging by her cuisine, she was a proud Levantine. Only later would this become an issue.

## WHITE BEAN AND TOMATO SOUP

Overnight, soak 2 cups (300g) of dried white beans in water with 1 teaspoon of baking soda. The next day, wash the beans well. Grate 5 ripe tomatoes and pass them through a sieve to remove the seeds and skins. Place the beans, grated tomatoes, 2 tablespoons of concentrated tomato paste, 1 finely chopped onion and ¼ cup (60ml) of olive oil in a large saucepan. Season with salt and pepper, add 1.5 litres of water and cook for 1½ hours, or until the beans are tender. Serve the soup piping hot with a spoonful of rice.

Joya and her elder sister Clara grew up in Haifa, on the shores of the Mediterranean. In the nineteenth century, a modern city started to emerge on the slopes of Mount Carmel, as both local authorities and European immigrants decided to invest in its development.[4] From a small seaside village surrounded by fig trees, fields of wheat and barley and green pastures dotted with cows and sheep, Haifa slowly grew into an important commercial city. German Templars, Russian wheat traders, French shipping companies and Austrian insurance firms were all attracted to Haifa's natural port. In 1908, the newly expanded commercial port became the only maritime outlet of the famous Hijazi railway, the massive enterprise of the Ottoman Empire connecting Damascus and Medina by over 1300km of iron tracks.[5] From 1800 to 1900, the city's population grew twenty-fold, from a mere one thousand to over twenty thousand residents, including an ever-increasing bourgeoisie.[6] For the Ben-Naim family, who traded in goods all around the Mediterranean, the growing metropolis of Haifa seemed the natural place to live.

In Haifa, the girls got a better education than the traditional schools of Tiberias had offered. Both studied at the Alliance Israélite Universelle school, which was part of a progressive and secular French organization with schools all around the Ottoman Middle East and North Africa providing advanced and often free multilingual education to boys and girls alike.[7] Twenty years earlier, Zion Asheroff had studied French, Arabic and Hebrew at the newly established Alliance school in Jerusalem. He, too, had been keen to get the sort of education that would prepare him for the modern world. Joya and Clara would have studied geography, French, literature and mathematics, as well as European history. Their education directed their gaze towards a life of independence and freedom, a life not limited to domestic chores and child-rearing.

At the Alliance school, Clara met Yosef Khalfon, the Arabic teacher. He came from a notable Haifa family who (perhaps like the Ben-Naims), originally from Tétouan in Morocco, had relocated to Tiberias in the 1860s and later settled down in Haifa.[8] The family, who counted some important rabbis among its members, enjoyed the protection of the French consul. In 1908, when Clara turned eighteen and completed her studies, she married Yosef and moved to Alexandria in Egypt. That same year, a revolution by the Young Turks, a political movement which aimed to replace the sultan's authoritarian rule with a multiparty democracy, established a new constitutional government in Istanbul, under the banner of 'Liberty, Equality, Fraternity and Justice'.[9] These political transformations caused instability in the Ottoman Empire which could be felt even in its minor provinces, such as Palestine. In moving to Alexandria, Yosef Khalfon might have thought it would be a good idea to relocate to a commercial city that enjoyed closer trade relations with the British and French empires. In addition, like many other young men in Palestine, he might also have been tempted to leave Haifa to avoid conscription into the Ottoman army, which from 1908 became mandatory for men of all religions.

After living in a small city like Haifa, Clara and Yosef must have been impressed by Alexandria, with its elegant cafés, wide avenues and rich cultural life. It was a thriving port city where merchants, travellers and poets mingled with the local cosmopolitan society.[10] Like the rest of Egypt, it was nominally part of the Ottoman Empire, but had been unofficially ruled by the British since 1882. Imperial expansion had brought new European communities to the city, alongside the Greeks, Jews, Muslim and Christian Arabs who had lived there for centuries. Clara and Yosef, who spoke Arabic and French, soon felt at home and continued to live there even when Yosef decided to open a stationery shop in Cairo, in the wealthy quarter of Heliopolis. They would continue to send beautiful postcards and heartfelt holiday greetings to their relatives in Palestine until the Second World War.

Back in Haifa, Joya became a charming and intelligent young woman ready for a life full of promise. Like her elder sister, she had attended one of Palestine's best schools, and would therefore have been prepared for a career if needed. And yet, her parents thought that her future would be best secured by marrying well. Joya turned nineteen at the end of the First World War, and it was time that she found a husband. Her choice, however, was clouded by the financial demise of her family. Like many other merchants in the Ottoman Mediterranean, her father's wealth dwindled during the war, when several important trade routes were severed. Yitzhak rarely talked about his mother's family, but from the fragmented information I've gathered, it was clear that the family's dire economic situation was enough to cast a shadow over the younger daughter's future.

We don't know exactly how or where Joya met Yehezkel Mizrahi, who was twenty-six years her senior. Yehezkel was the descendant of a family of merchants whose sons settled down in key commercial cities around the world, including Istanbul, Alexandria, Manchester and Los Angeles. A few years before their wedding, he moved to Jerusalem, where he had hoped to find not only new business opportunities, but also a bride. Joya was considered lucky to marry a wealthy man who would provide her with a prosperous future, but it's hard to read her feelings in the surviving photographs I have of the couple. In one, she leans lightly on his shoulder, her gaze one of detached aloofness. She seems seized by a desire to be elsewhere.

It is ironic that I know so little about Joya beyond the food she used to cook, because cooking was never her vocation. Had things gone according to plan, as the wife of a wealthy merchant, she would never have been expected to cook anything. She would have had hired help to take care of domestic chores, such as cooking and cleaning. But she had a strong sense of the flavours and scents that food should have. The stuffed red peppers should be firm and a little hot on the tongue, and the rice should be thoroughly cooked but never sticky. The mejadra should be covered with a generous quantity of fried onions, an amount that almost seemed to be too much but was in fact just right. None of her recipes had more than a few ingredients, but their flavours were strong, precise and decisive.

# MEJADRA

Take 1 cup (200g) of small dark green or brown lentils, rinse well and pick out any debris or shrivelled lentils. Put the lentils in a medium-sized pan, cover with cold water and cook over a medium heat until they are slightly softened. Add 1 cup (200g) of washed basmati rice, 1 cup (250ml) of water, a little olive oil and a pinch of salt and continue cooking. In a separate pan, fry 1 finely chopped large onion in plenty of olive oil until it is golden and crisp. Add the onion to the pan of rice and lentils, cover the pot with a lid and cook for a further 20 minutes over a low heat, until the rice and lentils are soft and all the liquids have been absorbed.

RECIPES HAVE ALSO GIVEN ME SOME INSIGHTS ABOUT Yehezkel's past, which is only sparsely recorded in official archives. Yitzhak told me that one of his favourite dishes was fassoulia, a bean soup that he often ate accompanied by rice. Another frequent dish was ful, a thick stew of slow-cooked fava beans made with fresh beans in spring, or dried ones in the winter, and drenched in fruity olive oil with a little salt but no other condiments. He also liked to have a dollop of ful on a plate of chickpea hummus with tahini. He enjoyed eating a lemony soup with meat and rice balls, celery and green herbs, which resembles an Arab dish called kobeba hamda, a name that Yitzhak never used when he cooked this soup for me.[11] All of these dishes are in fact typical of the Syrian Jewish community in Egypt. Yehezkel's brother, Nissim Mizrahi, ran the family import and export firm in Aleppo. Had Yehezkel also lived in Syria before moving to Jerusalem? The dishes he liked were migrants' food, simple and unpretentious, meals that a bachelor like Yehezkel could have bought at a restaurant in Cairo's market or at the port of Alexandria where Syrian migrants worked and ate. If I take Yehezkel's culinary legacy as hints about his past, the recipes seem to direct us to back to Aleppo, a home his family had left behind and which was never mentioned again.

## RICE AND MEATBALLS IN LEMON AND CELERY SAUCE

In a wide pot, cook 4 roughly chopped celery stalks (including the leaves), a roughly chopped bunch of parsley, the juice of 2 lemons, 2 chopped garlic cloves, 3 tablespoons (45ml) of olive oil, and season with salt and pepper. Add 1 cup (250ml) of water and bring it to a boil. Make the meatball mixture with 250g of minced beef, ¼ cup (50g) of basmati rice, ½ cup of finely chopped parsley, a little olive oil and salt and pepper. Mix well and form it into small balls. Place the meatballs in the sauce and add water if needed (they should be half-covered in liquid). Cover the pot with a lid and cook on a low heat for 30 minutes or until the rice is fully cooked.

IN THE FIRST YEARS OF THEIR MARRIAGE, YEHEZKEL continued to travel back and forth throughout the eastern Mediterranean. In his shop in Jerusalem, he sold precious textiles from Syria, delicate Egyptian cotton and fine English wool. He stocked beautiful cotton lace to adorn ladies' blouses and dresses, elegant handmade embroidered collars and colourful silk ribbons. Many people in Palestine saw the new century as the dawn of a prosperous new era.[12] There were opportunities to be exploited, a thirst for novelty and plenty as the population grew, the Ottoman rulers invested in infrastructure and culture, and the trade connections improved. Women wanted to dress more elegantly than ever, and Yehezkel's shop did well by selling them the latest fashions, both local and international.

When he needed to stock up on new fabrics and other goods, he could travel on the new railway all the way from Haifa to Damascus. The route passed through the Jezreel Valley in Palestine before connecting to the main line of the Hijazi railway and turning north at Daraa. The wood-panelled carriages were small yet included such amenities as a restaurant and a prayer room. It was a journey that Joya could also take comfortably, when she joined her husband on his business trips. The train could have taken them further north to visit his family in Aleppo, the city famous for stuffing anything: stuffed peppers with rice and meat, stuffed courgettes in lemon and garlic sauce, stuffed pigeons with pine nuts and herbs, stuffed tomatoes with lots of parsley and coriander. Were these dishes new to Joya, or were they similar to the food she had known from her childhood in Tiberias and Haifa? She didn't have the patience – or the passion – for complex preparations but the humble and forgiving peppers were easy enough to make and remained a staple dish in her household.

# STUFFED PEPPERS

Take 6–8 small light green peppers, slice their tops off (save them as lids to cover the peppers later) and empty out their seeds. Grate 8 ripe tomatoes into a pulp, and strain to remove the seeds and skins. Place the tomato juice in a large ovenproof pot, add 1 teaspoon of sugar, 1 small chilli pepper and a pinch of salt and simmer for 20 minutes. In a bowl, mix 1 cup (200g) of washed basmati rice, 250g of minced meat (beef or lamb or a mixture of both), generous bunches of finely chopped parsley and coriander, 2 tablespoons (30ml) of olive oil, and salt and pepper to taste. Spoon the rice mixture into the peppers so that they are three-quarters full, and put the tops back on them as 'lids'. Arrange the peppers upright in the sauce, and cook over a medium heat for 20 minutes. Preheat the oven to 170°C (gas mark 3). Put the lid on the pot and put it in the oven to continue cooking for 45 minutes.

YEHEZKEL AND JOYA WERE LEVANTINES, PART OF THE Ottoman world, people who moved around the eastern shores of the Mediterranean and lived in the shadow of empires.[13] He wore a fez and spoke Arabic and Ottoman Turkish, she spoke French and wore silk dresses. He invested his wealth in gold coins that did not lose their value even after the fall of the Ottoman and the

Austro-Hungarian empires. She filled her woven silver handbag with amulets against the evil eye. They belonged in cosmopolitan cities like Jerusalem, Haifa, Alexandria and Aleppo, where people of different religions, languages and nationalities were used to living together. I don't think that they would have realized that they were slowly becoming strangers in the places they used to consider home, as these hybrid Levantine cities gave way to sectarianism and nationalism.

Yehezkel and Joya married soon after the end of the First World War. During the war, the slow collapse of the Ottoman Empire had reverberated through Jerusalem, destabilizing the local economy. He was too old to fight but could still support the war effort by buying Ottoman bonds, even if their value seemed less and less secure. The price of gold rocketed alongside the rate of inflation, which rose by hundreds of per cent every month.[14] By 1915, the residents of Jerusalem could hardly afford to buy sugar, wheat, meat or vegetables when a plague of locusts decimated local produce and local and American relief funds offered free bread and milk to the poor. Initially Yehezkel's business seemed immune to the instability that shattered the Mediterranean commercial networks.[15] True, it became increasingly difficult to get fabrics, laces and ribbons from abroad, and local customers had less money to spend on luxury goods. But Yehezkel was a shrewd businessman, and he managed to get along.

The initial optimism faded quickly. The war bonds Yehezkel had bought – like all those who believed that the Ottoman Empire could never collapse – were, after its defeat, not worth the paper they were printed on. The British brought new fashions to Palestine, but the growing demand increased the competition, as new shops opened in Tel Aviv and Haifa, offering a wider selection of fabrics and lace. Spiralling inflation slowly consumed what was left of his money, leaving little to live on.[16] Within a few short years, Yehezkel became trapped in an unfolding economic disaster from which he saw no way out. Would the Mizrahi family have to rely on charitable offerings too?

To Joya, it must have seemed absurdly unfair that her husband, whom she had married in the hope of a life of comfort and ease, was now penniless. When he fell ill – perhaps as a consequence of the collapse of his business and livelihood – she was the one who had to take care of him, and their firstborn child, Luna. It is baffling to me that Yehezkel did not sell the gold coins that he had kept in the safe of a Jerusalem bank, which were only discovered long after his death. Losing his money and status, he seemed also to have lost the appetite to live.

After the fabric shop closed down, the Mizrahi family moved from their house near Jaffa Street to a flat in Yemin Moshe, a neighbourhood that had seen better days, having been built by the British Jewish philanthropist Moses Montefiore decades earlier. But even then they did not have a fixed address. 'It is cheaper to move to another flat than to paint the walls white for Passover,' Joya used to say. In the social and political order dictated by their new rulers, people like Yehezkel and Joya Mizrahi were pushed to the margins. From the British perspective, they were helplessly poor, 'Oriental' natives lacking in political connections. The rising Zionist nationalist movements, led by European immigrants, also had little consideration for the Jews of the Levant.[17] For a cosmopolitan merchant like Yehezkel, the freedom to move across borders mattered more than a national home, and now this attachment to mobility was frowned upon.

It was in the flat in Yemin Moshe that, in 1924, their second child, Yitzhak, was born. The burden of poverty was one of his earliest memories. All day long, his mother would cook, bake, clean the house, wash the linen and their clothing. She did it reluctantly – being poor was an insult – but she was now forced to take on the household chores which she should have been exempt from by dint of her education and her class.

Joya cooked cheap, nourishing meals that lifted Yehezkel's spirits, even if only momentarily. These humble dishes seem remote from the elegant, aloof figure in the photograph, in which she is standing in a silk frock and clutching an evening bag. These were not the dainty and refined dishes that she felt entitled to. But today, as much as I understand how she must have felt, the meals she cooked against her will seem simply delicious. Her cooking was the epitome of comfort food. She rarely cooked meat, and often preferred dishes that could be cooked in one pot. Fewer dishes meant less work. There was no proper stove in her simple kitchen, so she would place her large pot over a kerosene burner and slow-cook the daily meal. Every day, she made a fresh pot of fluffy white rice that could be spooned into the soup, or absorb the sauce of the stew. It was food that could be eaten with a spoon, from deep terracotta plates decorated with daisies or glazed a golden pink.

## RICE

Rinse and drain 1 cup (200g) of basmati rice. Heat 3 tablespoons of olive oil in a pot and stir the rice into it. Cook for a few minutes over a low heat until the rice is translucent. Add 2 cups (500ml) of water and 1 teaspoon of salt. Bring to the boil. When the water has almost all been absorbed, cover the pan with a clean tea towel and the lid, and steam over a very low heat for 10 minutes, or until the rice is cooked. Let the rice rest for 10 minutes before serving.

FOR YITZHAK, THIS FOOD OBVIOUSLY HELD MEMORIES OF home and family, but it was also an eternal reminder of failure and defeat. It was the food of a father who lost his wealth and a mother who lost her dreams, the food eaten in a cold house in the winter. He could not let go of these childhood memories and flavours, but he could never bring himself to translate those memories into words that could be shared with anyone else. He did his best to ignore his parents' origins, but could not persuade himself to give up their food.

# Chapter 7
# JOYA MIZRAHI IN JERUSALEM, 1932–1936

J OYA WAS FEROCIOUSLY SUPERSTITIOUS. S HE WOULD FILL the house with garlic cloves against the evil eye and throw salt behind her left shoulder to blind the evil spirits who lived there. Among the amulets she kept in her purse were little silver hands decorated with a crescent and a star of David, blue eyes, an ivory tooth and a small copper frog, all of which were supposed to keep the devil away. She also had a little enamel pendant of a bearded Moses holding the tablets of stone, which I now own and still like playing with. Nonetheless, forced to live in a small, cluttered and cold flat in Yemin Moshe, she thought she was very unlucky, tricked out of the destiny to which she felt she was entitled.

Yemin Moshe was established in a vineyard. It was probably not really a vineyard, but it was named the 'Vineyard of Moshe and Yehudith' by its founder, Moses Montefiore, who, with his wife, funded and supported the Jewish community in Palestine in the nineteenth century.[1] Yemin Moshe was built in his honour, one of the first Jewish neighbourhoods outside the walls of the ancient city. It was a cluster of square, two-storey stone houses set along steep narrow streets, originally planned to house about 120 families but soon accommodating many more. Montefiore preferred constructing elegant villas for the middle class rather than homes for the poor. But at the turn of the century, the expanding Jewish community of Jerusalem crowded the streets of the city, and many were forced to move out to the more spacious and hygienic – but also less protected by the municipal police – neighbourhoods across the valley, returning daily to the city centre to work and shop at its markets and workshops.

After their financial catastrophe, the Mizrahi family rented a cheap flat in one of those small stone houses, just a couple of rooms with a tiny kitchen at the back. There was no stove or running water. The streets of Yemin Moshe face Jerusalem's original city walls, and its residents witnessed from across the valley how British planners transformed Jerusalem into a mythical 'Old City', divided it into quarters and made it a living museum of Judaeo-Christian civilization and kept any modern novelties at bay.[2] When I walked up and down in the neighbourhood's paved streets, I found it hard to imagine how it might have been a century earlier, its streets unpaved, the houses unkempt and some in ruins after the 1927 earthquake. Now, it is impossible to ignore the beauty of its upscale stone houses; they were remodelled in the 1970s to host artists but soon became too expensive for them and now appeal mostly to foreign real-estate investors. Unlike the Bukharan Streets – where the decrepit palaces are but a shadow of their one-time glory – this modest neighbourhood now glows with quaint elegance. The poverty-stricken families that for decades had populated these streets are long gone and forgotten.

For most of the twentieth century, the neighbourhood remained a frontier zone that could be easily cut off from supply and communication lines, as would happen all too often during conflicts. No wonder that living there made Joya feel like an exile. In Yemin Moshe, self-sufficiency was vital. Local flour, patches of vegetable gardens between the houses, water wells and pasture for grazing cows promised independence for the community. The old communal windmill, built by English engineers to guarantee flour supply to the inhabitants, became the neighbourhood's symbol. By the time the Mizrahi family settled there, however, the windmill had stopped functioning and flour was produced by modern steam mills.[3]

The busiest place in the neighbourhood was the communal bread oven. It was operated by the baker who made fresh bread every morning and special cakes for holidays and celebrations. On Fridays, he would open up his oven to accommodate dozens of small clay pots containing the local women's Sabbath casseroles. Each woman would send her own dish to bake overnight and would pick it up the next morning for lunch on Saturday. One of these pots has found its way to my kitchen, where I look at it with awe, too stunned by its antiquity to use it. My pot is deep red terracotta, small and round, with two side handles and covered with a little matching lid. It would have contained the usual weekend preparations of sofrito or cholent, both forgiving dishes that could accommodate a variety of ingredients according to the season, the economic situation or the cook's skills and provenance. There were pots of chicken and beans, macaroni and meat, barley and potatoes. Sometimes, Jerusalem artichokes would be added to the mix. Joya's version was usually simple: potatoes, spicy meatballs or chunks of meat, some black pepper and bay leaves, some cinnamon. After long hours in the oven, the lid was lifted to reveal a miraculously scented, deep brown stew. She would serve it with her usual fluffy white rice that enhanced the flavours and absorbed the sauce.

# SOFRITO

Take about 6 medium yellow potatoes, peel and cut them into 1.5cm-thick slices. Heat some olive oil in a pan or casserole and fry the potatoes until both sides are golden. Remove the potatoes from the pan and put aside while you prepare the meat. Take 400g of beef cubes (preferably braising steak cut into 4cm cubes) and sear them in the pan. Add 4–5 halved shallots, 4–5 bay leaves, some whole black peppercorns and a generous spoonful of ground cinnamon. Arrange the potatoes on top of the meat and season abundantly with more cinnamon. Add some salt and pepper, a generous splash of olive oil and enough water to cover the meat, but not the potatoes. Continue to cook on the stove with the lid on for about 1 hour, adding more water if it starts to dry out. As an alternative, if you use an ovenproof casserole, you can slow-cook it in the oven at 100°C (gas mark ¼) for at least 5 hours, or overnight.

THE BAKER'S OVEN SPREAD WARMTH IN THE COLD JERUSALEM nights. It was a place of encounters between people of different lands and languages, natives and immigrants, all cooking together, sharing recipes and gossip. Yemin Moshe was originally divided into Sephardi and Ashkenazi zones, but in practice the neighbourhood's daily life was one of generous harmony.[4] Life in a poor and forgotten no man's land generated a sense of solidarity among the residents that transcended their cultural, culinary and linguistic differences and gave rise to a thriving sense of community. Yet Joya never enjoyed these oven-side conversations. Perhaps she didn't feel that she belonged among the Ladino-speaking women, who would not understand her French nor appreciate her aloofness, and nor would she have felt at home among the Eastern European Yiddish-speakers. Instead she would send Yitzhak to place the clay casserole in the baker's large oven, and to collect it, warm and heavy, the following day. Yitzhak, who grew up among Greeks and Poles, Yemenites and Bulgarians, Jews and Arabs, was used to hearing a mixture of Hebrew, Russian, Ladino, Arabic and Yiddish in the streets. Jerusalem absorbed its residents' distinct histories and made everyone, in one way or another, local.

Whereas Joya responded to the challenges that life presented her with by retiring into the privacy of her home and refusing any contact with the world outside, her son's strategy was different. Yitzhak felt at home in Jerusalem, in a way that this parents never did. He would tell me about his youth in Jerusalem and how he had set about exploring his native city in order to find his place there. He wanted to be a great man, but he wasn't sure how.

Yitzhak's attraction to Jerusalem was not religious or nationalistic. He admired its historical importance and avidly read about the rulers who had fought for it and the pilgrims who gave up everything they had to see its treasures. Unlike his parents, who saw themselves as Levantines who chose to live in Jerusalem as one of many accommodating cities in the region, his sense of identity was defined by his place of birth. He would walk down Julian's Way (today King David's Street) from Yemin Moshe to the city walls, and stroll from the Jaffa Gate by the Citadel through the old city with a natural ease. He spoke Arabic with the vendors in the market and with those who prayed by the Dome of the Rock. He made life-long friends with merchants and priests whose families had lived there for generations. He felt at home wandering through the labyrinth of narrow streets in the Maghreb neighbourhood to see the impromptu markets, the Western Wall or the Armenian monasteries. He saw beauty everywhere and continued looking for it even where it was mostly hidden from sight.

In Jerusalem, Yitzhak first cultivated his greatest passion – markets. He loved looking at the abundance of goods offered for sale, absorbing the atmosphere of constant exchange, inhaling the scents of unknown foods he hadn't tried before. Throughout his life, the market – or, in its absence, the supermarket – would be the first place he would visit in a foreign city, to gauge its spirit and absorb its traditions. In Jerusalem, the market stalls lined up by the walls, where bakers, cooks and fruit and vegetable vendors invited him to buy bread and spicy olives, tomatoes and lemons, fresh cheese and sweet sesame halva.

At the market, he first discovered the savoury ring-shaped cookies, flavoured with sesame, fennel seeds or with mahlab, a spice made of ground cherry seeds, that would become his favourite. The spices each gave the cookies a different flavour, whether it was earthy or sweet, sharp or bitter. At another stall he would eat 'Turkish salad', or ezme, made with peppers and onions cooked in tomato sauce, served with a thick slice of bread. Years later, he sought to replicate these recipes in his own kitchen with a passion that as a child I did not understand. Now I see that it was an attempt to revive the taste of his first independent explorations of the city he loved.

## TURKISH SALAD

Blanch 5 ripe tomatoes quickly in boiling water, then peel and grate them, removing as many seeds as possible. Cut 1 light green pepper, 1 red pepper and 1 medium-sized aubergine into large cubes. Finely chop 1 small onion, 2 garlic cloves, ½ a chilli pepper and generous bunches of parsley and coriander. Place all the ingredients into a large pan, seasoning it all with salt, ground black pepper, a pinch of cumin and hot paprika to taste. Add 2 cups (500ml) of water and cook for 45 minutes over a high heat, or until the vegetables are soft.

In the Machane Yehuda and Agripas markets, not far from the Jaffa Road in the western part of the city, Yitzhak ate dishes that would accompany him for the rest of his life: rough, everyday food eaten by local labourers, both Arab and Jewish. They were meals that promised to keep you healthy and strong, ready for hard work. There were thick pieces of sizzling herb omelette fried in olive oil eaten between two thick slices of bread. There were bowls of thick dried pea soup with rice, or lentil stew with tomatoes and onions that would warm him on a winter's day for only a few pennies. There were steaming hot fried falafel, made with chickpeas or fava beans, yellow or green, spicy and crisp. Yitzhak was not yet thirteen, but from then on he would choose to cook and eat the food he had first tasted in his childhood.

## FALAFEL

Overnight soak 1 cup (150g) of dried chickpeas in cold water with ¼ teaspoon of baking soda. The next day, drain and rinse the chickpeas. Finely chop (or use a food processor) a large onion, 2–4 garlic cloves, a slice of dry bread soaked in water, and a large bunch of coriander, and mix it into a paste with 3 tablespoons of water. Season generously with salt, ground dry coriander, ground cumin and hot paprika to taste. Finely grind the chickpeas (using a food processor or a meat grinder) and add them to the herb mixture. Heat plenty of oil in a pan for deep frying, and scoop balls of the mixture into the hot oil. Fry the balls until they are golden brown and leave them to cool slightly on a rack.

IN THE EARLY 1930S, JERUSALEM WAS CHANGING QUICKLY. A shrewd observer, Yitzhak cannot have failed to notice the swift increase in immigration from Europe. Within a decade, almost a quarter of a million Jewish migrants moved to Palestine. The rise to power of the Nazi regime in Germany, and its violent persecution of German Jews, led tens of thousands of them to leave their homeland to settle in Palestine. Other Jewish immigrants arrived from Poland, Austria and Czechoslovakia. Many of them were secular, middle-class professionals, driven by Zionist ideology to participate in building a 'Jewish national home' in Palestine.[5] Some of the wealthier immigrants established new factories in Tel Aviv and Jaffa that contributed to the industrialization of the hitherto predominantly agricultural Palestinian economy. Even if the local Jewish society in Palestine did not immediately welcome the newcomers – their habits were often viewed with suspicion – in the long term, they gave a boost to the local Jewish economy and culture, and reached dominant positions in society.

The arrival of thousands of migrants from Europe created new social divides between 'Western' and 'Eastern' Jews.[6] The distinction between Ashkenazi and Sephardi or Mizrahi communities was hardly new, but the place of the Palestine-born Jews remained unclear. For the Eastern European Zionists, they were too local, too closely intertwined with the Arab Palestinian society, too attached to the past that Zionism wanted to reinvent. The Palestinian Jews themselves often challenged Zionism's nationalistic vision of progress, which was inspired by Western political ideologies, and sought a way to reconcile Jewish sovereignty with the multinationalism that characterized the region.

People like Joya and Yehezkel, as Levantine and Ottoman Jews, slowly became foreigners without ever being displaced, as the places they inhabited changed hands. The concept that each individual should carry one nationality, ideally the one they were born into, seemed inconceivable to them. But it was deeply impressed in the mind of their son, Yitzhak, who grew to resent his parents' fluid identity. He realized that the very idea of what it meant to belong had changed radically, and he felt responsible for the future of his mother and younger brother. He decided that it was better to evade specific definitions. Only later, when the struggle within Jewish society became evident and the Ashkenazi community seemed to have the upper hand, would he associate himself with the winners.[7]

As Yitzhak and his family tried to find their place in the new Jewish society, their lives were transformed by the intensifying conflicts between the Jewish and the Arab populations. In 1929, a series of summer demonstrations in Jerusalem escalated to violence. By 1936, the tensions had erupted into what the British described as the 'Arab revolt'.[8] Six months of general strikes led to ferocious attacks against both British and Zionist people and property. The clashes increased in 1937 after the British Peel Commission recommended the partition of Palestine and the founding of two separate states, one Jewish and one Arab.[9] The commission proposed that the Jewish state would control large territories in northern Palestine, where many Arabs had lived for generations, and was met with vast Arab opposition and resistance. Each party in the struggle had its own interpretation of the events: for some, the revolt was an anti-colonial insurrection, others saw it as an Arab nationalist revival in opposition to the rise in Jewish immigration, yet others highlighted the complaints of the Arab peasantry, who did not profit from the industrial initiatives that Jewish immigrants brought to Palestine.[10] Years later, when I asked Yitzhak about the revolt, it seemed impossible for him to recall how he and his family had felt at the time, except through the overdetermined lens of subsequent events. In Yitzhak's mind, the memory of violence erased decades of peaceful coexistence of diverse communities in Jerusalem.

The growing hostilities might have been what finally led the Mizrahi family to leave Jerusalem, but it is also possible that they moved because of financial difficulties, or because of the tragedy that had struck them. Yitzhak's elder sister, Luna, fell ill with scarlet fever during one of the frosty Jerusalemite winters of the early 1930s. For weeks, Yitzhak watched Luna lying in bed, her body getting weaker and weaker. Despite her mother's care and the doctor's remedies, she succumbed to her illness, and was buried in the Mount of Olives Cemetery in Jerusalem. Her traumatic loss continued to haunt Yitzhak for the rest of his life.

As the archives maintain an insistent silence about them, it is hard to be certain of the reasons why, or even exactly when and how, the Mizrahi family left their home. Their names are missing from the lists of residents in Jerusalem, from the Sephardi community's archives, and only appear, unexpectedly, in a 1935 list of names that were to be removed from Jerusalem's electoral roll.[11] Here they are, finally noted in official records. Joya is thirty-six years old, and her husband is sixty-two. Their address is listed as a rented room in a house belonging to someone else, in a poor neighbourhood not far from the Bukharan Streets. The archives tell me nothing more. But I know that sometime between 1936 and the outbreak of the Second World War, they packed their belongings and travelled west, towards the sea, to Rishon LeZion.

For the first time, the Mizrahi family would live in a village whose inhabitants were all Jewish Zionists. Rishon LeZion was founded in the late nineteenth century by Zionist immigrants from Russia and Eastern Europe who bought a large stretch of land south of Jaffa and sought to establish an agricultural settlement. Baron

Edmund de Rothschild funded its promising winemaking industry, planting vineyards and establishing a large-scale vinery.[12] With palm-lined streets and unassuming detached houses, it had little of Jerusalem's charm or of its urban liveliness. The local community was small and close-knit, often unwelcoming to newcomers. Perhaps the natural plenty that surrounded the Mizrahi family's new home would now provide the calm and security they had hoped for. Yet in a place that glorified agricultural work, Yitzhak remained a city boy.

In the old cemetery of Rishon LeZion, now a sprawling city of white cement towers, I located the tomb of Yehezkel Mizrahi, son of Kamar. The tombstone marks the year of his death, 1941. When Yehezkel died, in the midst of a world war, sixteen-year-old Yitzhak officially became the family's breadwinner. He had to drop out of high school to support his mother and younger brother, and he found a job watering orange and almond groves. He passed his days among the trees, with the other workers, who were mostly Arab. The bittersweet scent of almonds and citrus kept him company in the long hours under the scorching sun. When harvest time came at the end of the summer, he loved sitting in the shade and eating the delicious almond kernels.

During the Second World War, living in an agricultural settlement had its advantages: when other parts of Palestine suffered hunger and strife, the family had a steady local supply of fresh fruit and vegetables. With almonds from the local trees – and some eggs and butter from the neighbouring farms – Joya would bake a cake as nutritious as a whole meal, which Yitzhak ate in thick slices.

# NUT CAKE

Grease a rectangular cake tin (23x12cm) with butter and dust with plain flour. Preheat the oven to 180°C (gas mark 4). Beat 3 eggs with ½ cup (125g) of sugar until they are light and creamy. Using a spatula, fold in ½ cup (60g) of plain flour, 1 teaspoon of baking powder, 2¼ cups (275g) of mixed ground almonds, hazelnuts, walnuts and pecans, according to your preference. Add the zest of 1 lemon, and ½ cup (120g) of cool melted butter. If you would like to add fruit, fold in 50g of sultanas. Pour the mixture into the tin, place it in a hot oven and bake for 45 minutes, or until the cake is set and browned.

Yitzhak, his mother and brother lived in Rishon LeZion like strangers: they had little or no money, they didn't know anyone, and did not interact with local society. They felt as if they were exiled from the bustling and multicultural urban life that they were used to. As soon as the war was over, Yitzhak became impatient to leave. He decided that the family should settle down in the big city, in Tel Aviv.

## Chapter 8

# ESTHER ADIRIM IN RIGA, 1928–1941

I WAS WALKING DOWN ELISABETH STREET IN RIGA, ON A bitterly cold November day. The wind was blowing as I stopped to look at the beautifully ornate Art Nouveau buildings that made this street famous. The faces of mythical creatures and cascades of stone-carved flowers stared at me from the elegant facades, next to minimalist modernist blocks with geometric gables and large windows. I could understand why interwar migrants from the Baltic countryside found Riga so appealing: it blends modern elegance with Nordic cosiness. Among these immigrants were my paternal grandmother, Taube, her parents, Esther Simanowitsch and Abram Adirim, and her six siblings. In 1928 they all settled down in a modern apartment on Lāčplēša Street, on the outskirts of the old city, near the Jewish school.[1]

Esther and Abram had been married for over twenty years when they moved to Riga. She was born in 1886 to a family of gold merchants from Kovno (today Kaunas) in Lithuania, and he was born in 1880 in Rēzekne, a town east of Riga, where his family owned a soda-water factory. I am not sure how they met: theirs seems an unlikely union. But since Abram's father's family also originated from the Kovno region, the marriage could have been arranged. Abram was a dreamer and a reader, always ready to joke and discuss the political news of the day. Esther was stubborn and austere, uncompromisingly following the family traditions she had been brought up with. No photograph of them as a couple survives; the only one I have is a collage of their two portraits, glued together by an invisible hand.

In the Latvian archives, I discovered that Abram's and Esther's ancestors had moved freely around the Baltic region of the Russian Empire, taking advantage of the imperial provinces' porous borders, both seeking economic opportunities and escaping anti-Semitic persecution.[2] Abram and Esther also moved from place to place. They first lived near Abram's family in Rēzekne in Latvia's Latgale region. In 1909, after a couple of years there, they moved 25km nearer Russia, to Ludza (Lyutsin in Yiddish), a pretty lakeside town with small wooden houses and unpaved streets that hosted a large community of Lithuanian Jews, including renowned Talmudic scholars.[3]

The Adirims' wooden house stood on Pushkin Street, just two blocks from the lake.[4] Like all of Ludza's houses, the central room was the kitchen, with its warm stove and large table, around which Esther's children ate, played and studied. To feed her growing family, she relied on simple recipes from Latgale's traditions and from those of her own family back in Lithuania. Her cooking was based on few condiments and fresh seasonal ingredients. In the long winter, she would cook soups from thick barley groats or tangy white cabbage, served with dense dark rye bread. For Esther, no meal started without a soup, and she passed this principle on to her children.

# BARLEY GROATS SOUP

Originally, this soup was made using barley groats, until pearled barley groats became more widely available. Pearled groats have a more delicate flavour, but are less nourishing. Soak 1 cup of groats in cold water overnight. The next day, drain the groats and place them in a large pot together with 1 halved onion, 3 peeled and roughly chopped carrots and 3 chicken thighs. Add enough water to cover everything. Bring the pot to a boil, skim the surface, and cook for about 1 hour over a low heat. Now remove the chicken (it can be boned, shredded into strips and returned to the soup, or eaten separately) and add 3 peeled and quartered potatoes. Cook the soup for another 30 minutes, add salt and pepper and serve hot.

IN THE SUMMER, THEY ATE FRESH COTTAGE CHEESE MIXED with rich cream, small buckwheat pancakes with wild berries, and crunchy green cucumbers from their vegetable garden. Salted sprats were more common on their table than the expensive fresh carp from the nearby lake. The carp was reserved for the holidays, when Esther turned it into gefilte fish, mild-tasting patties served in their own cool aspic, later popularized by East European Jewish migrants in the United States. In Ludza, gefilte fish was not a mythical emblem of Jewishness but a simple healthy way of cooking fish, using both the flesh and the bones to enhance its nutritional value. Gefilte fish was eaten throughout the Baltic, Poland and Russia, but while the Polish version was sweet and the Lithuanian one peppery, in Latvia, the flavour of the fish itself was allowed to shine. In Esther's kitchen, it was this version that prevailed.

## GEFILTE FISH

Grind about 1kg of fresh carp without the head or tail, but with the bones to make them more nutritious. If you prefer a more delicate taste, you can remove the bones. You can also ask your fishmonger to grind the fish twice for a smoother texture. Keep the fish heads, tails and bones (if you haven't included them) for the sauce. Add to the ground fish 2 very finely chopped onions, 2 eggs, about 3 tablespoons of sugar, 1 tablespoon of salt, and 1 teaspoon of freshly ground black pepper. The mixture should be strongly flavoured (Esther used to taste a little on the tip of the fork). Add about ½ cup of matzo meal or breadcrumbs and mix well to get a soft but not runny mixture. Let it rest while preparing the sauce. In a large pot, cook the fish heads, tails and bones with 2 halved onions. Peel 4 carrots, cut them into round slices, and add them to the pot. Add enough water to cover the fish (too much water will make the sauce too runny) and season with another tablespoon of salt, 1 tablespoon of sugar, and black pepper to taste. Bring the sauce to a gentle boil and simmer for 15 minutes. While it is cooking, form the fish into patties, and then place them gently into the sauce, in multiple layers if needed, but making sure that they are mostly covered with liquid. Lower the heat, cover the pot and continue to cook for 1½ hours. Transfer the patties and the sauce to a dish and cool in the fridge overnight (the sauce will set and turn into aspic). Serve cold with a spoonful of aspic, a slice of cooked carrot and a dollop of chrain.

ESTHER HAD LIVED IN LATVIA FOR ALMOST A DECADE WHEN she became Latvian. After the collapse of the Russian Empire, Baltic nationalists established republics in Latvia, Estonia and Lithuania.[5] Esther was given Latvian citizenship, like her husband. If she had any reservations about it, there was little that could be done; by law, a woman had to take her husband's nationality after their marriage. Her extended family in Kovno now lived in a different country and she was formally separated from them by a national frontier. From then on, Esther's life would be signposted by border crossings. Jukiškis, Eglaine, Joniskis, Meitene: the stamps on the pages of her yellow, crumbling passport, which I recovered from the Latvian archives, prove that she passed through the border that divided Riga and Kovno multiple times. The demarcation line had little meaning for people like Esther, who saw the expansive countryside of the Baltic as their home. Wide golden and green fields dotted with ice-blue lakes, thick forests and medieval villages were the landscape of her youth. The crisp potato cakes she was especially fond of were ubiquitous throughout the region, albeit with distinct local twists: fried in goose fat in Poland, covered with ground black pepper in Lithuania, or served with fresh soured cream and cucumbers or red berries in Latvia. Did such local traditions amount to a 'national' cuisine? I am not sure that Esther would have understood the question.

## POTATO LATKES

Roughly grate 1kg peeled yellow potatoes and one large onion. Add 4 tablespoons of plain flour and season with salt and ground black pepper. Heat some oil in a pan and carefully spoon in heaps of the potato mix. Flatten the patties with the back of a spoon, and fry on both sides until they are golden and crisp. Fry the latkes in batches to avoid overcrowding the pan. Cool the latkes on a rack and serve hot with sour cream or apple sauce.

MOVING TO RIGA OPENED UP NEW OPPORTUNITIES FOR the Adirim family; in 1928 the city's population was more than ten times bigger than that of Rēzekne and fifty times bigger than Ludza's.[6] It was a cosmopolitan modern metropolis, a bustling city where Latvian, German, Russian and Jewish cultures could – for a short while at least – peacefully coexist. The young Latvian republic launched a policy of cultural autonomy for minorities and established new schools where students were taught in Yiddish and Hebrew.[7] Riga became a major centre of trade in the Baltic, exporting meat, dairy, and even grain to its neighbours. As a result, it attracted thousands of peasants and merchants from the countryside, who populated the expanding city's newly built apartment blocks.

The Adirim family quickly integrated in the life of Riga. Abram worked at one of Latvia's many socialist Yiddish newspapers. Jewish publishing companies were thriving in interwar Riga, and within a few years the family were able to move into a comfortable flat in a large neo-classical condominium in Stabu Street. When I visited, a neighbour told me that the street was notoriously also the location of the KGB headquarters during the Russian occupation. Today, the building houses a museum documenting the interrogations and torture that took place behind the elegant facade, just a few blocks down the road from the Adirims' flat. But in the early 1930s, Stabu Iela was a good address, at the heart of a new neighbourhood, close to important synagogues, dance halls and schools.[8]

The Adirim family would have been welcomed to Riga by some familiar faces, such as Abram's widowed mother, Gena-Rivka, who had moved there a few years earlier. She settled down a few steps away from the market at 17 Elijas Street. Next door to her building was the Byelorussian synagogue, where she met a Mr Schapiro who worked there. I don't know very much more about him or their marriage. All I could find in the archives was Gena-Rivka's passport photo.[9] In it, she looks tiny, her smiling face wrinkled like a walnut, her hair combed into a little bun. When I was in Riga, I tried to find their address but none of these houses exist any more; the synagogue and adjacent buildings were burned down by the Nazis on 4 July 1941 and replaced after the war with new anonymous blocks.[10]

Apart from Mr Schapiro, no one in the family seems to have been especially religious. In Riga, Abram led a secular life and took pride in his socialist Zionist positions. No pork was eaten at his dinner table, but neither did he follow other kashrut laws with any particular zeal. His sons, Selik and Harry, married their wives in civil ceremonies at the town hall rather than in the synagogue. By the early 1930s, Riga was the heart of the Zionist movement in Eastern Europe, and Abram became more interested in ideological debates about Jewish politics than in religion and tradition. The newspaper where he worked provided him with a constant flow of information about political groups, local visits by eminent politicians and heated discussions about the future of Jewish society in Latvia and beyond.

Esther, according to her passport, was a housewife. In her modern kitchen, she passed her days cooking meals for her children (there were now eight), their friends and fiances, and the neighbours and relatives who would often drop by in the evening. In Riga, the kitchen's typical centrepiece would be the cast-iron wood-fired cooking stove.[11] There were colourful ceramic tiles on the walls, decorated with a geometric pattern, and floral enamel plates and pots. The kitchen had a single sink and a single oven, with no distinct sets of cutlery or plates for dairy and meat. These traditional features of Jewish kitchens were unnecessary in the secular Adirim household. Any feelings of religious reverence had been left behind in Ludza or Rēzekne and seemed wholly inappropriate in liberal, cosmopolitan Riga. Instead, as a nod to bourgeois aesthetics, Esther bought a special set of plates for fish, decorated with paintings of various local water creatures. The kitchen was certainly better equipped than the one in their previous house in Ludza, but there was no vegetable garden or nearby forest where she could forage for mushrooms and herbs. Instead, Esther had to cross the old city centre and shop at Riga's new covered market.

Housed in former zeppelin hangars, the local market that opened in 1931 was the largest in Europe.[12] Every day, hundreds of trucks and carts arrived from the countryside to provide the city with a vast selection of dairy, meat, fish and vegetables. At their orderly stalls, vendors in white aprons sold fresh rye bread and scented pickles, sweet butter and thick cream, hot tea and salted herring, retrieved from large strong-smelling barrels directly in front of the customer.

I walked to the market from Stabu Iela, trying to see the sights Esther might have seen on her shopping trips. I strolled down the main street, which Esther would have known as Marjias Iela, after Maria Alexandrovna, the empress of Russia. In 1991 it was renamed for Riga's dissident poet Alexander Čaks, whose poetry depicts life in Riga in the 1930s, the time when Esther lived there. Later, in the British Library in London I found a rare English edition of his poems, a small red book illustrated with modernist etchings of urban scenes.[13] Even in translation Čaks's verse captures the spirit of Riga's urban landscape of lifts and high-rises, cinemas and music halls, taverns and bars, trams and shops, workers and capitalists.

Čaks's poetry is – perhaps surprisingly – full of food: pink slices of melon and baskets of red apples, a butter-yellow moon and dark bread night, summer radish and plums, smoked herring and Dutch cheese, sparkling seltzer water and bitter beer, and plenty of ice cream. Through his poems, I can almost taste interwar Riga, where Esther lived and cooked. I can see and smell Marjias Iela, with music pouring out of its French-style cafés and lights shining bright in its sweetshops. Imagining Riga at its most vibrant, it is difficult to believe that its progressive promise would be so fragile and short-lived.

When I finally reached the market, I realized it was still gigantic, almost exhaustingly so. There are endless rows of small shops and open stalls, with fresh fish and seafood, piles of green herbs and cabbages, large plastic containers full of everything that can possibly be pickled, from brightly coloured vegetables to small briny fish. The market has become a tourist attraction – so much so that the stallholders have put up signs banning photographs. An Uzbek baker invited me to try his bread, which smelled exactly like the bread I had eaten in Samarkand. But although the market is still alive, it feels curated – like an exhibition in a museum. I wonder if Esther found the market's extraordinary abundance satisfying or confusing. Perhaps she preferred the impromptu stands set up outside the hangars, where local farmers came up to town to sell their produce in the open air, next to the long lines of flower stalls. Esther could have filled her shopping cart with potatoes, onions and a piece of fresh beef, which were enough to make one of her family's favourite lunchtime dishes.

## MEATBALLS IN ONION SAUCE

Make the meatballs by mixing 300g of minced beef with 2 finely grated large onions, 1 egg, 2 tablespoons of crispy breadcrumbs or matzo meal and season with salt and pepper. Form the meat mix into small balls.

In a medium-sized pan, fry 1 large chopped onion in 2 tablespoons of oil until it turns golden. Add 2 cups (500ml) of chicken stock, season it with salt and pepper and bring to a boil. In a small bowl, mix 2 tablespoons of flour with 2 tablespoons of water until it's smooth, and add it to the sauce, whisking energetically to prevent lumps forming. Gently arrange the meatballs in the sauce. Cover the pot and cook for 30 minutes, and serve with mashed potatoes.

MODERN RIGA HAD MUCH TO OFFER TO THE ADIRIM children. Roha-Taube (usually shortened to Taube), who was just five years old when the family moved to the city, grew up to be a sociable, independent girl, whose life was shaped by the rhythms of the city rather than by tradition or religion. She could stroll on her own between the busy tramway cars and the residential avenues, wander in the city's blooming parks and skate with friends at the Esplanade ice rink. She shared her father's political passion and, at the age of ten, joined the socialist Zionist youth movement, Hashomer Hatzair, which trained local youth for emigration to Palestine. Every Saturday she went camping in the forests surrounding the city or to Hebrew lessons. She admired the stylish new music halls and went with her brothers to concerts and ballets at the legendary national opera house. In the interval, they would buy delicious cheesecake and milky tea. Taube could dream of a future that her mother could not even imagine, one that promised her not only all the entertainment Riga had to offer, but freedom too.

# BAKED CHEESECAKE

Make a dough by mixing 280g of plain flour, 3 tablespoons of sugar, 3 egg yolks, 120g of softened butter, 2 tablespoons of oil, 1 teaspoon of baking powder and 1 teaspoon of vanilla extract. Wrap the dough and put it to chill in the fridge for 30 minutes. While it is chilling, make the filling by mixing 500g of whey or light white cheese, 1 egg, 70g of sugar, 50g of raisins, 1 tablespoon of corn starch, 1 teaspoon of ground cinnamon and the zest of 1 lemon. Grease a rectangular cake tin (about 20x30cm) with butter and dust with flour. Now take three-quarters of the dough, roll it into a thin sheet and place it in the tin to cover the bottom and the sides. Pour the cheese mixture onto the dough base. Preheat the oven to 180°C (gas mark 4). Use the remaining dough to make a decorative trellis and place it carefully on top of the cake. Put it in the oven and bake for 45 minutes or until the dough is golden and the filling is set.

THE ADIRIMS WERE NOT ALONE IN SEEKING NEW opportunities in Riga. Between 1920 and 1930, the city's population doubled to over 300,000 people. Thousands of Jewish families wanted to leave the poor rural eastern region of Latgale; those who did not move to the United States, South Africa, England, Australia, Canada or Palestine settled in the capital. Riga's dense medieval centre and its more modern suburbs could barely contain the constant flow of migrants. The city's limited size, its growing population, its narrow streets and closed courtyards were a recipe for dirty, unhealthy air. As a result, every summer thousands of city-dwellers – including the Adirims – would escape the pollution and take the train to the seaside resort of Jurmala.

Jurmala is not a place exactly, but an idea: in Latvian, it simply means the 'seaside'. Once a string of fishermen's villages, in the nineteenth century Jurmala became the quintessential summer outpost of Riga's residents. Only the more affluent bourgeois families would have their own dacha by the sea, but everyone who could afford it would rent a house or a couple of rooms in a 'pension' and spend June or July breathing the sea air and taking long walks along the peaceful waterfront. The houses of Jurmala were surrounded by orchards of apricots and plums, as well as plentiful wild bushes of raspberries and blueberries for the visitors to pick and eat. Esther used the plums and the berries to make a sweet and tart compote that she would keep in glass jars to enjoy in the cold winter months. Preserves were not only a way to use up the abundant summer fruit, but also a memory of the lazy joy-filled days of the Baltic midsummer.

## SUMMER FRUIT COMPOTE

Take about 1kg of mixed summer fruit (apricots, peaches, berries, plums). Remove the pits, and cut the larger fruit into halves or quarters. Place them all in a large saucepan with 150–200g of sugar (to taste) and the juice of

2–3 lemons (depending on the fruit's sweetness). Add enough water to cover the fruit and cook gently for 45 minutes, or until the fruit is soft. Store the compote in the refrigerator and serve cold.

IN FEBRUARY 1934, ABRAM DIED. HE WAS ONLY FIFTY-FOUR years old. The death certificate I found in the archives records the cause as heart disease, angina pectoris. For the first time in her life, Esther had to find work in order to support her three youngest daughters, Taube, Luba and Sima. Abram's colleagues at the newspaper found her a job in the distribution department, and her older children probably helped too. Selik and Harry were now tailors. Leib was about to graduate from high school. Haja had married a Mr Brenaizin from Lithuania and lived with him in Kovno, not far from her aunt and uncle. Scheina worked as a nurse at the local hospital. For ten-year-old Taube, the loss of her adored father was devastating. She didn't get along with her stubborn, distant mother, but she had been close to her father, who had always known how to make her laugh. As the eldest daughter in the house, now that he was gone and her mother was going out to work, she was expected to take her mother's place and cook for the family.

Reluctantly, Taube took charge of the kitchen. She prepared dinners of chopped liver with pickles, carrot tzimmes, or the noodle kugel that her mother and her younger sisters liked, but her mind was elsewhere. She started at secondary school, the Jewish Gymnasium, where she excelled in Yiddish grammar and biology, and in the afternoons, she gave private Yiddish lessons to younger children in her school. She was still a member of the Hashomer Hatzair, where she enjoyed participating in political debates. She dreamed of following her sister, a nurse, into the world of medicine, setting her sights on becoming a doctor. But she felt that her opportunities were limited by the demands her mother made of her. Money was short, so to help make ends meet, she took an afternoon job as a tailor's assistant, mending the elegant suits of Riga's Jewish bourgeoisie. Taube disliked sewing even more than she disliked cooking, but she was quick to learn and soon started to make her own clothes in her spare time. A checked woollen coat, a velvet dress with faux-fur lining, a dark blue blazer and skirt. If she was forced to sew, at least she could make all the garments she could no longer afford to buy.

## CARROT TZIMMES

Peel 8–10 large carrots and cut them into thin strips. Place the carrot strips in a saucepan and add enough water to cover them. Add 1 teaspoon of salt and some sugar – about ¼ cup (50g) or more, depending on your preference. You can substitute some of the sugar with honey, or thicken the sauce by adding a little bit of flour mixed with some water. Stir the sauce well to avoid lumps and cook for 30 minutes or until the carrots are soft and the sauce thickens.

THE YEAR 1934 WAS TRANSFORMATIVE NOT ONLY FOR THE grieving Adirim family but also for the Latvian republic and its citizens. After just fifteen years of democratic government, the politician Kārlis Ulmanis – one of Latvia's 'founding fathers' – staged a coup and launched a nationalistic dictatorship.[14] An early admirer of Benito Mussolini, he took inspiration from the fascists' rise to power in Italy. The generous minority rights that made Riga a safe haven for many communities were abolished. The result was violent anti-Semitic attacks, the closure of Jewish Zionist newspapers and youth movements (including Taube's Hashomer Hatzair, although it continued to meet clandestinely), and daily arrests of Jewish leaders and politicians.

The repercussions were immediate, and very close to home. Did the Adirims feel personally intimidated? Did they care about the demise of democracy? Esther's electoral record shows that she voted in the 1928 general elections, and again in 1934, in a national referendum on old-age, disability and unemployment insurance. Yet her family in Kovno, Lithuania, were denied the vote and had lived peacefully under authoritarian rule since 1926. Her daughter, Haja, had even moved to Kovno in 1933. The region had been ruled by emperors or dictators for centuries. Democracy was the exception, not the rule.

Even if one notices the signs of political collapse, it can be hard to decide what measures to take in response. Sometimes only an instinctive decision, or sheer luck, separate certain death and random salvation. In Latvia, there had been debate about nationalism and national identity since the country's independence in 1918. Did it really matter that, in the name of nationalism, the parliament was disbanded? After all, the Adirim family was as Latvian as anyone else, at least formally.

After the coup, when cultural minority rights were outlawed, everyone – even simple housewives – was expected to show their allegiance to Latvia. The nationalistic attitude manifested itself even in cookbooks published under the new regime, which sought to instruct Latvians how to cook, host and entertain in the 'Latvian way'.[15] One suggested that decorating the table with linen cloths and meadow flowers was distinctly Latvian, as were dishes such as boiled pig's head, beans, peas and sauerkraut. Another insisted that sweetness was not a crucial feature of Latvian cooking, as imported sugar had become too expensive. Another very popular book of recipes – a guide to 'practical cooking' – explained how to make everyday Latvian staples. Milky soups, cold salads, salted herring and stuffed cabbage leaves were heralded as the true heritage of the Latvians, to be distinguished from Russian, Prussian or Polish traditions. Was Jewish cooking even considered 'Latvian' any more, or did the ban on pork – such a key ingredient of Latvian cuisine – exclude Jews from the national cauldron?

I doubt that the Adirims asked themselves whether their cooking was 'Latvian' enough. Esther's food, seasoned lightly with dill, onion, caraway seeds, salt and cinnamon, was simple and traditional. She mitigated the sharpness of her pickled cabbage and herring with tart sour cream and rich cottage cheese. She balanced the richness of her chopped liver with a pickled cucumber or a dollop of deep red chrain, a hot sauce made with beetroot and horseradish that brought tears to the eyes of whoever ate it. She made potato salad with pickles and mayonnaise which was similar to the Russian Olivier salad that was eaten not only in Latvia but all around the region. Absorbed as she was by the challenges facing a widowed mother struggling to pay the bills, questions of national allegiance were hardly her priority. But all around her, politicians were chanting 'Latvia for Latvians' while either nationalizing or shutting down Jewish businesses and social organizations. Political identity and national belonging were no longer theoretical.

## POTATO SALAD

In a pan of water, boil 3 potatoes until they are cooked but still firm. Allow them to cool, and then peel and cut them into 1cm cubes. Boil a couple of peeled carrots until they are soft, and dice them into small cubes. Mix the diced potatoes and carrots with 2–3 chopped pickled cucumbers (in brine) and add 1 tablespoon of mayonnaise and a pinch of salt. You can also add some finely chopped dill or parsley, or a chopped hardboiled egg, if desired. Refrigerate the salad overnight before eating.

By the end of the 1930s, Taube felt as if everyone was leaving. Abrasha, her first boyfriend, was preparing to emigrate to Palestine, where his mother and sister had settled a few years earlier. Taube's scout leader Shmulik also moved to a kibbutz there, leaving his family behind while he realized his Zionist vision. He invited Taube, and the rest of the group, to join him. Esther would not hear of emigrating, least of all to distant Palestine. Remarkably, the Latvian archives revealed to me that she had a passport, and signed it in Hebrew.[16] Her name, Esther Adirim, was written in loose Hebrew cursive, very different from her husband's graceful Cyrillic signature. In a later passport, from 1939, a neat bureaucratic calligraphy claimed she was illiterate and therefore could not sign the document. It's tempting to read the lack of signature as an act of resistance against an increasingly violent state, or a statement about her true identity. Until that point, Esther had evidently used her Hebrew signature openly, seeing no need to hide her Jewishness. After that, though, even she sensed the imminent threat in the air.

After war broke out in September 1939, Latvia declared itself neutral and started to export food to keep the economy afloat.[17] As the country sent its best grain, butter and meat to Russia and Germany, food in Riga was rationed. At the huge market, Esther could only find scraps. Government propaganda claimed it was a time of national sacrifice to maintain Latvia's independence. We now know, however, that Latvia's future had already been sealed by the Molotov–Ribbentrop pact, the secret protocol by which the Soviet Union claimed its interests in the Baltic region. But in the warm summer of 1940, Taube was as surprised as everyone else in Riga to see Soviet tanks moving into the city centre. The 200,000 Red Army soldiers were welcomed by some Latvians as friendly defenders against Nazi Germany, but most decried the Soviet occupation as the end of the country's short-lived liberty.

In September that year, Taube returned to the gymnasium as usual after the summer holidays. But now all classes were taught in Russian. Every week, students would disappear, and rumours suggested that they and their families had been deported to Siberia. The national opera house reopened, but with a repertoire approved by the regime. Taube and Abrasha could still find standing tickets for the ballet, where they were able to observe

Russian officers in uniform and their consorts in cheap silk dresses sitting in the stalls. They would still go ice-skating at the rink, but no longer sat at the local café, which now served the new rulers with sliced oranges covered with fresh thick cream.

I know little about Abrasha, except that he played the piano, loved the opera and ballet and came from a wealthy family. No photos of him and Taube in Riga survive, but the bond between them was as strong as teenage love can be. Abrasha must have been just seventeen when he was caught by a Russian officer with a letter from his mother in his pocket. A letter written in a foreign language – Hebrew – was, for the Soviet regime, a strong enough proof of treason. This, at least, was the explanation for his arrest that Taube heard from their common friends, but in fact no real proof was needed in 1940 for arrest and deportation in Riga, and thousands of others ended up in Siberia for no reason at all.[18]

After his arrest, Abrasha was put on trial, declared an enemy of the people and swiftly deported to Siberia in a cattle-train. His father tried desperately to get him back, but his bribes served for nothing. Abrasha was just one of many – almost a quarter of the Jewish community of Riga disappeared without trace in the Soviet gulags. Those who avoided deportation were enlisted into the Red Army, like Taube's elder brothers Selik and Harry, whose wives and children had to move in with Esther and her daughters. The flat in Stabu Street became a safe place where all the Adirim women gathered, cooked and ate together, trying to resist the strife outside.

The last sign of the family in the Latvian archives dates from 22 July 1941, twelve days after the Nazi invasion of Riga, when the housing register records that they all fled to Russia.[19] About five thousand Latvian Jews had done the same, many evacuated by the retreating Red Army and later sent as workers to collective farms or labour camps.[20] But the Adirims' story was not as simple as that. Esther didn't want to leave, so they were not evacuated. Taube used to say that her mother insisted that 'at least in Riga they had a roof over their heads'. The thought of spending the rest of her life on the road, travelling through unfamiliar countries, or being forcibly settled in a Russian *kolkhoz*, frightened Esther very much. She shrieked at the idea that her sons would return from the war to find an empty house. She insisted on ignoring the crumbling city, the empty markets, the disappearing neighbours and friends, and held on to her home as the last vestige of honour and respect: anything was better than being a refugee.

But when the news came that the German occupation of Lithuania had begun, sixteen-year-old Taube gathered all her powers of persuasion to convince her mother, sisters and sisters-in-law to take the last train out of Riga's central station. It would not be forever, she insisted, just a quick escape to the safety of the Russian countryside. On a humid, rainy afternoon at the end of June 1941, they left their flat to board the train, then slowly travelled across the familiar golden fields of Latgale, where Abram and Esther had made their first home.

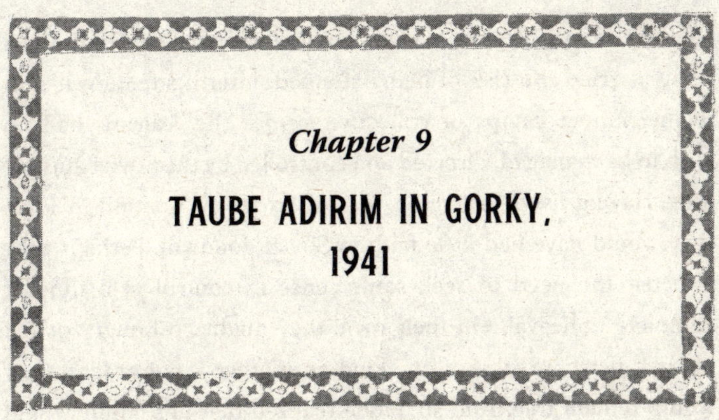



# Chapter 9

# TAUBE ADIRIM IN GORKY, 1941

IN 1932 STALIN RENAMED THE CITY OF NIZHNY NOVGOROD after its most famous son, the writer Maxim Gorky. When I read in his autobiography about his grim childhood by the Volga river, I understood why Gorky himself preferred to live in the Italian riviera.[1] By the Second World War, Gorky was the third largest city in Russia and the central manufacturing base for MiG aircraft and submarines. It was also a city of soldiers and spies, where tens of thousands of Red Army recruits, from all around the Soviet Union, lived in vast military barracks, undergoing basic military training while waiting to be sent to the front. This is why Taube had brought her family to Gorky: her brothers Selik and Harry were stationed there, and she was determined to convince them to desert.

Riga and Gorky are 1,350km apart. In the 1930s, this trip, a twenty-four-hour train journey in the best of times, would take the traveller via Moscow, on the railway line that crossed the Soviet Union from west to east. During the war, this was not an advisable route. Moving along the main transport lines of the Red Army carried the risk of being stopped, interrogated, even sent to internment camps or collective farms. The Adirims had no wish to be managed, directed and controlled by the Soviet authorities. Having lived through a year of Soviet occupation in Riga, they would have had little faith in Soviet goodwill. Perhaps they also felt the need to seek some sense of control at a time of complete upheaval. On their own, they might go hungry or fall ill, or suffer hardships of one kind or another – but at least they would remain free. And so Taube realized that her family would have to disappear.

When the Adirim women had boarded the train at Riga station on a damp day in late June, they were among thousands of others who feared that this was their last chance to escape before the Nazis arrived. As they rattled eastwards, Taube looked out as the city shrank behind them, its buildings soon replaced by villages and green fields.

Near the Russian border, the train stopped, although they didn't seem to have arrived anywhere. At first Taube assumed there was a technical problem, but talking to the other passengers she learned that the border was closed. Esther, Taube and the rest of the family sat close together in the train carriage, trying to figure out what to do next. They watched from the windows as thousands of people, mostly women, children and elderly men, in their best clothes and clutching suitcases with their most precious possessions, descended the train and sat outside, waiting in the damp afternoon. Would it be safer on the train, or in the fields? They did not know how long they would have to wait.

Although it was getting late, Latvian summer evenings are never

22. Zion Asheroff
holding his grandchild.

23. The Asheroffs in Petah Tikva during the Second World War.
Sitting, right to left: Shlomo-Haim, Hananya, Eliachar, Zion,
Penina and her son Eddie with their cousins.

24. Zion and Batya-Hannah Asheroff
in Petah Tikva, early 1940s.

25. The Asheroff family, early 1940s. Bottom left: Hananya and Zoulay; by the table: Zion and Batya-Hannah, holding the photos of their absent daughters, Penina and Tzvia.

26. The Blue Bird Café in Petah Tikva.

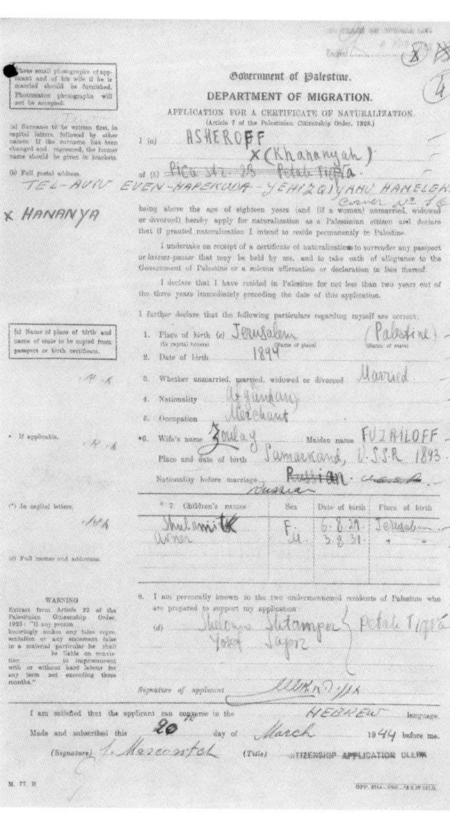

27. Hananya Asheroff's application for Naturalization Government of Palestine, 1944.

28. Passport photos of Hananya and Zoulay Asheroff, 1944.

29. Hananya Asheroff's Certificate of Naturalization by the Government of Palestine, 1944.

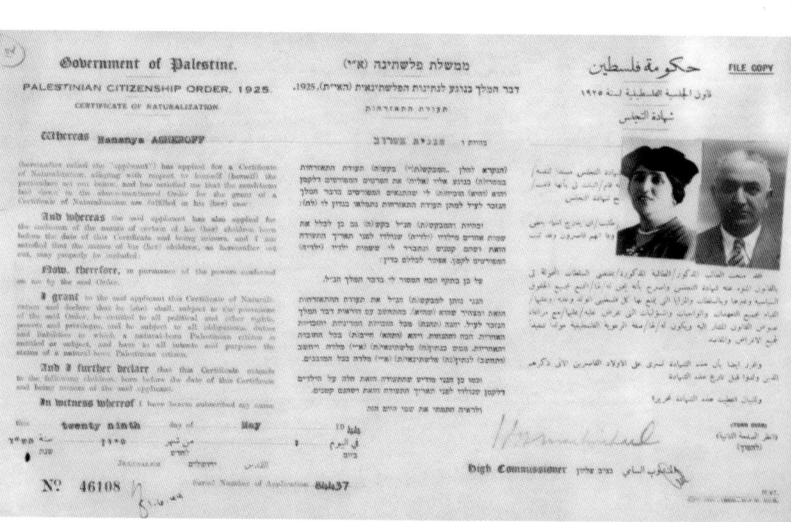

30. Shulamit and Yitzhak visiting the conquered Arab village Ein Karem in Jerusalem, summer 1948.

31. The Yavne Jewish School in Bad Reichenhall DP Camp, 1947. Selik Adirim's son Hatzkel was among the pupils.

32. A house in Bad Reichenhall DP Camp, c. 1946.

33. Tova and Isaac Rosenboim
in Tel Aviv, 1950s.

34. Shulamit and Yitzhak Efrati
at a party, 1960s.

35. The Efrati house at 21 Kehilat Odessa Street, Tel Aviv.

36. The Asheroff house in Jerusalem, 2023.

37. Shulamit, Ilana and Or, 1995.

38. Tova and Or, 2015.

really dark. Thousands of people sat on the ground, under a cloudy deep blue sky, uncertain what to do. Blazes of red and orange appeared between the clouds and illuminated the horizon: the German Luftwaffe bombing the villages by the border. Taube could hear women screaming and gathering their luggage and crying children. The panicked masses, disorderly and breathless, began to walk towards the Russian border.

The Adirim family also got off the train and advanced, slowly, towards the checkpoint where armed soldiers kept guard: an old matriarch, a young mother, two pregnant women, three teenage girls and four toddlers. Esther surely thought that she had been right to dread the destiny that awaited women and children on the road, and they hadn't even left the country yet. Somehow Taube was confident that this was still their best choice, but to everyone else the whole trip must have seemed like a terrible mistake, and it was too late to go back now. They moved towards the checkpoint, where four soldiers stood firm. Next to the family, two stout men dressed in fur coats led their horse and cart to the gate and joined the queue.

The crowd grew restless as rumours started to spread that the Germans were advancing quickly from the south. Maybe these voices reached the soldiers as well, or perhaps they were ordered to open the gate and let everyone in. It was almost dark, and Taube could hardly see the soldiers who shouted at her to stop. 'Who needs the cart more? You, or them?' one soldier asked the two men who also approached the gate. 'The cart must go to the women and children,' another soldier decided, handing Taube the reins. She helped her mother, sisters, sisters-in-law and nephews to climb up, then sat on the bench, and the horse pulled the cart slowly down the road to Russia.

As I followed the tale of the family's escape to a safety of sorts, it became evident that it's a story about hunger. Everyone was hungry, then: the Adirim women, the displaced people they met on the way, the local residents, everyone. This was hardly unique – throughout history humanity has suffered from long periods of scarcity and famine. But living through this ordeal meant that sourcing, preparing and consuming food was the continual over-riding concern. Just as she had been at home, Taube was in charge of the kitchen. Every evening, when the cart stopped at the side of the road, Taube would cook a simple meal: cabbage soup, vegetable broth with dried noodles, potato latkes fried in a drop of oil. Even when food was scarce, she insisted on making something that resembled a proper meal. With only one aluminium pan, a grater and a bonfire – if they were lucky – it was hard work. But chopping, grating, frying and boiling the familiar food of home gave Taube a sense of purpose at a time of despair and chaos. Sitting on the cart at sunset with her sister Scheina, her sisters-in-law Sara and Sara, and their small children, all sharing enamel bowls of hot soup, Taube could pretend that normal life might, after all, be restored one day.

## CABBAGE SOUP ON THE ROAD

Finely chop a medium-sized white cabbage (about 500g) and 1 onion. Saute the onion with 1 tablespoon of oil until it is lightly golden. Add the cabbage and cook for a further 5 minutes. Add 2 tablespoons of concentrated tomato paste (optional) and 2 tablespoons of sugar, then season with salt, pepper and a hint of sweet paprika. Add about 400g of drained sauerkraut (pickled cabbage, either tinned or home-made), mix it all well and cover with 1 litre of water. Cook the soup for 45 minutes, or until the fresh cabbage is soft.

TRAVELLING BY CART WAS A BLESSING, BUT IT MEANT using some of the family's meagre portions of carrots, cabbages and oats to feed the horse just enough to keep going. Food was scarce and stopping to get more was risky. Raw potatoes left rotting in the field might have tempted hungry children, who would not have known that they were poisonous, even deadly. When Esther became weak from malnourishment, Taube exchanged her coat for a loaf of bread. Hunger was constant, inescapable.

The roads east were packed with older people and young families who walked from one village to another in search of food and shelter, only to discover that the German air raids had left everything in ruins. In fact, even approaching any human dwelling was a huge risk, as planes continued to fly over them, searching for targets. The Adirims took the side roads, slowly circumventing not only the main junctions but also any signs of habitation. Every day, Taube would stop the cart to pick up those who could not walk, the elderly, the children and the wounded. They would share a ride and a meal, exchange potatoes and stale bread, rest for a while. They were complete strangers, with nothing in common except that they had been forced to abandon the lives they had built and take to the road. It was enough to tie them together and provide them some silent consolation for all they had lost.

Whatever food Taube found had to serve many, and last a long time. If they were lucky enough to get a little flour, and perhaps an egg, she would mix them into a batter diluted with water to make paper-thin blintzes that could be fried with a drop of oil and no more. Their one pan was so thin that it dented if used clumsily, and would have to be hammered back into shape, but it was light to carry and reliable enough for cooking on the road.

Blintzes filled with cheese, folded and fried in oil until crisp, were a staple dish in Riga, served with apple sauce or sour cream. At home the Adirims always served them as a main course, rather than dessert. I don't know if they were lucky enough to find any white cheese to fill their blintzes on the road. They were used to cheese that was strained of excess liquid, thick and firm, and sweetened with a little sugar or jam. But they now had to make do with whatever they could put their hands on. A little cheese, a stewed apple, a tiny bit of sugar, or nothing at all.

# BLINTZES

### (the full recipe)

The day before, make a batter with 3 cups (375g) of plain flour, 5 egg whites, 2 egg yolks, 3 tablespoons of oil and a pinch of salt. Gradually add 4 cups (1 litre) of water to make a liquid batter. Refrigerate the batter overnight. The next day, make a filling with 750g of white cheese (whey cheese is ideal, but cream cheese or ricotta would also do), about ¾ cup (180g) of sugar (or less, if it's too sweet for you), a little cinnamon and 2 tablespoons of cornflour or vanilla custard powder. Using a paper towel, lightly oil a frying pan. Heat the pan and pour some of the batter in so that a thin layer covers the whole pan; pour any excess back into the batter bowl. Cook the pancake on one side only, then turn it out onto a surface covered with a tea towel. Repeat the process until you have used all the batter. Next make the blintzes by putting 1 tablespoon of filling in the centre of each pancake, then fold it like an envelope: from the bottom upwards, then left to centre, right to centre, and finally close the top towards the centre. When all the blintzes are filled and folded, let them rest for an hour. When you are ready, heat some oil with a knob of butter in a frying pan, and fry the blintzes until they are crisp and golden on both sides. Serve them warm.

In order to preserve their independence, what could have been a twenty-four-hour train journey from Riga to Gorky became a three-month exodus on isolated country roads. When Taube could finally see the lights of Gorky on the horizon, she left the horse and cart at a nearby hospital, and the whole family settled down in a small guesthouse, not far from the military barracks. Wartime Gorky was a meeting point for refugees, clandestine travellers and perhaps even spies interested in its large tanks and weapons manufacturing plants. In the autumn of 1941, just as the Luftwaffe started bombing the city – leading to large-scale destruction – Taube began to work out her daring plan to save her brothers' lives against all odds, and against their will.

One Sunday morning in late September, Taube and Selik's wife Sara walked into Gorky's enormous military camp. It was visiting day, and the base was full of women and children searching for their fathers, sons and brothers in the cold yard. Taube scanned the crowds and eventually spotted Selik smoking a cigarette on his own. He was surprised to see his wife and sister, whom he expected still to be in Riga. Taube forced into his hands a long wool skirt and floral shawl and urged him to put them on, and quickly. A straightforward, practical man, he immediately understood what she had in mind.

While Selik was getting ready, Taube searched for Harry. She had expected that silent, reliable Selik would accept her improbably audacious plan, but Harry was a different kettle of fish. Good-looking, well-groomed and soft-spoken, he had his father's idealism, but lacked his initiative and his willpower. At twenty-two, Harry had married Sara, his first girlfriend, who had already been expecting their first baby. In Riga he had found a job as an assistant tailor, settled down with his wife in a flat next door to his mother, and he and Sara had gone on to have two more children. Even in the chilly yard of a crowded military camp, he looked sharp and shiny in his well-ironed uniform.

When Taube pushed a skirt and a shawl into his hands, he hesitated. Deserting meant stepping out of the respectable life he had always lived. If they caught him, the Russians would shoot him on the spot. The army offered Harry a better hope of salvation and dignity than he would find as a renegade soldier on the run. And he had been stationed in Gorky for months and had yet to fight for even a day. Maybe he would be among the lucky ones who came through unscathed. There was little time to come up with convincing arguments, but Taube repeated what seemed to her to be obvious: Harry belonged with his wife, his children and his family, not in the army of an oppressive foreign power. Harry, however, could not bring himself to wear the skirt and the headcover. He stood by the building in silence for a while, and when Taube pressed him to make up his mind, he decided to stay.

Taube rushed back to Sara and Selik, and the three of them headed out, desperately hoping that no one would stop them. They kept walking quickly and calmly, until they were through the checkpoint at the gate, then returned to the guesthouse where the rest of the family waited anxiously. Having to explain, especially to Harry's wife, why there were three of them and not four must have been difficult.

Taking the train out of Gorky was too dangerous, especially for Selik, as the station was notoriously packed with army agents seeking deserters. Instead, Taube found a local farmer who agreed to drive them to a nearby town in his open truck. As they drove, she felt her cheeks reddening with frost in the icy wind, relieved to be getting away from the city before winter buried it under a thick layer of snow. None of them were dressed for the cold; they had left Riga in haste at the summer's end. When the truck reached a small railway station in the outskirts of the neighbouring town, they got off, taking first a train to Kazan, then another one to Chelyabinsk.

It would have taken them several days to reach the dull, industrial city of Chelyabinsk. The streets were lined with banks of snow and Taube saw people queuing for cups of hot water, in a desperate attempt to keep warm. The city's factories produced tens of thousands of tanks, engines and ammunition, and were staffed with thousands of people whom the authorities purposely relocated there from all over the country. Soviet Russia was crumbling under the persistent German offensives, and Chelyabinsk, or Tankograd, seemed to care more about arms and tank production than about feeding its residents.[2] Having travelled east for more than 2,700km, Taube now decided it would be best to change route and head south. The next day, the Adirims boarded a train heading towards Kazakhstan.

The railway route from Chelyabinsk to Central Asia passed through places that had hosted innumerable travellers for centuries. The Kazakh steppes, rendered slightly more accessible to foreign visitors by Imperial Russia's railway network, were still a land of nomads and merchants, people who were used to living on the road. From the frost-covered windows of their wagon, Taube could see limitless snowy-white plains, and imagined them blindingly green in spring, and mild yellow in summer. She had never ventured so far away from home before. The landscape might have appeared foreign to her, but it was governed by Soviet Russia, just like Latvia. Taube had strongly opposed the violent Soviet occupation of her motherland, resented the oppression and fear that the Russian soldiers had imposed, and disliked the mandatory Russian classes at her school. Yet this despised imperial impulse of the Soviet Union gave her family the precious opportunity to escape. They didn't need to cross borders or ask for permits; they could simply disappear.

The Adirims must have been relieved to leave behind the war-torn cities for the silently welcoming desert. They continued to travel, with no set destination, looking for a sign that would tell them to stop. Then, in the midst of the long train journey south, somewhere in the Kazakh desert not far from the Uzbek border, Taube's older sister Scheina realized that her baby was imminent. Taube helped her off the train and the stationmaster accompanied them to a small, dirty hospital in a nearby village. Before they left the train, they agreed to meet the rest of the family in Tashkent in a couple of weeks.

## Chapter 10
# THE ADIRIM FAMILY IN LENINABAD, 1942–1946

A HISTORY OF DISPLACEMENT IS A TRICKY STORY TO TELL: in hindsight, the long and meandering route can easily be traced on the map, stops on the way can be pinned down and the destination clearly marked with a red flag. But the women of my family who made this trip in the winter of 1942 had no mental map of their journey, nor even a precise idea of their destination. The same was true for almost all those fleeing war and enemy bombs. They moved forwards, hoping to leave the dangers behind, but never truly certain of finding safety. The lucky ones had a small suitcase with some personal belongings that made the trip a little more comfortable, but most people on the road carried almost nothing, as they crossed unfamiliar landscapes, surrounded by strangers, hoping to find salvation.

Scheina's recovery from childbirth was slow, and she, Taube and the newborn baby finally arrived in Tashkent six weeks after the rest of the family. They found a city swarming with people: migrants, evacuees, refugees. The relief of having escaped the battle zones in the north-west was soon replaced with confusion.

They wandered the city, looking for shelter, uncertain how – if ever – they could find the others.

After two decades of Soviet rule, wartime Tashkent was a different city from the one that Zion and Hananya Asheroff had known. In the 1920s and 1930s, tens of thousands of people in the new republics of Uzbekistan and Tajikistan had been forced to emigrate. The wealthy merchants feared that their property would be expropriated – or 'nationalized' – or that they would be violently attacked for being 'anti-revolutionary'.[1] Many crossed the Amu Darya river to Afghanistan, leaving behind their houses and a civilization that had endured for a thousand years, but which seemed to have come to an abrupt end. The Russian authorities forcibly transferred other communities to Central Asia – including more than a hundred thousand Koreans – in their stead. When Taube and Scheina arrived there, Tashkent was on its way to becoming an industrial Soviet administrative capital: there were no sprawling blocks of modern buildings yet, but its small and crowded whitewashed houses were surrounded by factories and wide boulevards in the Russian imperial style, dotted with tall trees.

Since Tashkent was conveniently far from the war front, it soon became a centre for managed migration.[2] Initially, the Soviet authorities appeared to be engaged in a humanitarian project to evacuate people they sought to protect, among them the poets Anna Akhmatova and Alexander Watts and the composer Dmitri Shostakovich. They were joined there by tens of thousands of refugees. To the dismay of the locals, widows and orphaned children filled the streets, looking for a place to stay, a plate of hot food, a hint of information about their lost relatives.[3] The Adirims hoped that Tashkent could be a potential haven for them as well.

Scheina found a job as a nurse in the maternity ward of the

local hospital, which offered to take in her baby daughter as well, but refused to accommodate Taube, who spent her days looking for casual jobs in the local bazaar. When I visited Tashkent, the market was my first stop. More than seventy years after Taube walked around Chorsu bazaar, and over a century after Zion Asheroff helped his father to sell their textiles there, I finally saw it too. Now, however, it was hosted in a modern blue-domed structure, built by the Soviets after the devastating earthquake of 1966. The stalls were neat and orderly, shining in the early-morning sun. A gas oven produced heaps of delicious-smelling round flatbreads. Hungry workers sat down for a plate of shashlik or mantu dumplings in the large restaurant, sipping hot tea from blue cups. Brightly dressed women sat by piles of thinly sliced carrots or baskets of white and purple mulberries. There were heaps of dried summer fruit: sweet-smelling apricots and peaches, succulent persimmon slices, long strips of melon, plump brown raisins. I passed tables covered with herbs and spices, green coriander and golden saffron, red chilli peppers and ripe pomegranate seeds in their crimson juice. I doubt that Taube saw such plenty in the winter of 1942, when scarcity and hunger reached even the fertile agricultural land surrounding the city, and the competition for food was fierce.

Taube had high expectations of the bazaar: she hoped to find a job, new contacts, maybe even information about the whereabouts of her family. When nothing worked out, she sold her gold ring – a gift from her uncle, the Kovno gold merchant – for a few roubles and went to the railway station. At the ticket office, she asked where two people could travel for fifteen roubles. The cashier handed her two tickets to Leninabad.

The ancient city of Khujand, which the Soviets renamed in Lenin's honour, was founded by the Persian Empire on the banks of the river Syr Darya more than two millennia ago. It was conquered by Alexander the Great, who aptly renamed it 'Alexandria Eschate', Alexandria the Furthest.[4] Taube and Scheina would have agreed that Leninabad was remote: it was far from their Baltic home, far from the front line of the war, 110km south of Tashkent. Once a major trade hub on the Silk Road, it was a Tajik city of magnificent domed mosques, plentiful bazaars and fertile orchards in the foothills of the Zarafshan mountains. They found it welcoming.

In 1942, Taube and Scheina could sense only mild echoes of Khujand's past artistic and political glory, deeply transformed by twenty years of Soviet rule. The city's Tajik poets and scholars, along with many shopkeepers, artisans and merchants, had escaped in the 1930s, fearing Soviet persecution.[5] In their place, the Soviet government settled Russian citizens who had been sent from other regions of the Soviet Union to work at the city's collective farms, or *kolkhoz*. During the war, these migrants were joined there by many displaced people in search of a safe place to live, some of whom had travelled from as far as Poland, Germany and Ukraine.[6] Although there were Soviet evacuees and refugees in the city, there were fewer than in Tashkent, easing the competition for food and shelter.

Scheina was again able to secure a job as a nurse at the local hospital, and Taube sought her luck at the market. This time, she not only managed to find some food to buy, but she also met a group of young Jewish men from Riga. They shared a large room in town and invited her to stay with them. In normal times, a young woman like Taube would not have accepted an offer of hospitality from a group of unfamiliar men. But this time, Taube had no other options, and she accepted. She probably felt safe with her new hosts, with whom she shared a past: they had danced and skated in the same music halls and ice rinks in Riga, eaten the same cheesecake and red berry jam on summer holidays in Jurmala. Now they were all escaping for their lives, in a city far away from home. They could also protect her from the unwanted attentions of other men, who could easily become aggressive towards a young foreign woman.

After a few weeks, though, Taube and Scheina had saved enough money to rent a kibitka, a simple round wooden structure covered with mud. For the first time in months they had a house of their own. The kibitka had an open hearth to cook on and a hole in the ceiling to let the smoke out. There were two mattresses on the floor, some rugs and bed linen, and little else. There, Taube, Scheina and the baby set up home and started cooking again.

In her new kitchen, Taube made a lokshen kugel, a simple cake of thick noodles mixed with beaten egg and breadcrumbs, a little sugar and cinnamon, then fried in oil or butter in a small casserole. Warm and crisp, it was a Jewish import from northern climates, unheard of in Central Asia. For the Adirims it was a rare delight, unmatched even by the sweetest dried melon the market could offer.

## LOKSHEN KUGEL

Cook 250g of flat wide egg noodles (you can use pappardelle, but break them into small pieces before cooking) in boiling salted water until they are soft. Drain the noodles and rinse them in cold water. Leave them to cool and dry. Then, in a large bowl, mix the noodles with 2 beaten eggs, 100g of sugar, 2 tablespoons of matzo meal or breadcrumbs, cinnamon to taste and a pinch of salt. Heat some oil or clarified butter in a large non-stick pan, and pour the noodle mixture in to make a cake 3cm thick. Fry it until it is golden brown on both sides. If you use a smaller pan, you can divide the mixture into smaller quantities. Let the kugel cool a little before cutting it and serving it warm.

HAVING FOUND A PLACE TO LIVE, TAUBE NOW HAD TO figure out how to make it feel like a home. I don't think she really cared about blending into the environment. Whenever she could secure the ingredients, Baltic dishes would be served at the sisters' table. When she came back from the market with carrots – which the locals use to make palao – she made tzimmes. If she triumphantly brought home a head of white cabbage, Scheina would grate it into fine shreds for a cabbage and carrot salad or a warm cabbage soup. Whether it was the need to find some stability at a time of displacement, a suspicion of Tajik cuisine, or the simple pragmatism of cooking recipes with which they were familiar, the Adirim sisters cooked the food they had grown up with.

## CABBAGE AND CARROT SALAD

Cut a medium-sized white cabbage into quarters, and trim the ends of three large carrots, then grate the cabbage and the carrots using the coarse side of the grater. Add 1 tablespoon of sugar (or more if you prefer), the juice of 2–3 lemons, 2 tablespoons of mayonnaise, a little oil and some salt. Mix everything well, preferably using your hands. Taste it and adjust the seasoning if necessary.

EVERY MORNING, TAUBE WOULD WASH, GET DRESSED, MAKE her bed, and then sit down to write dozens of letters in a desperate attempt to find the rest of the family. She wrote to the Red Cross, to Jewish communities in Central Asia, to war aid agencies. There were so many refugees in the region that her efforts seemed useless. Months went by, and still she had no response, no sign of life.

While waiting for news, Taube found a job as a waitress in a small restaurant near the bazaar. Such places were not considered appropriate for decent women, but the trade-off was that food was always available, even if in modest quantities and with little variety. Taube served the customers the local version of plov (or palao) made with yellow carrots, cashews and hardboiled eggs instead of meat, prepared by an old cook in an iron *kazan* over an open fire. The diners were all men: workers in the market, wealthier evacuees or Soviet officers stationed nearby. There were no women at the restaurant at all, except for Taube and the other waitresses.

# TAJIK PALAO WITH YELLOW CARROTS, CUMIN AND EGGS

Hard boil 4–6 eggs (one per person), cool them in cold water and shell them. Heat 50g of clarified butter in an iron pot, add 2 chopped onions and fry them gently on a low heat until they turn golden. Add the eggs to the pot, on top of the onions, together with 8 carrots peeled and cut into strips and 70g of cashew nuts. Sprinkle with 1 teaspoon of cumin seeds and 2 teaspoons of salt. Do not stir the pot, but add 2 cups (400g) of washed and drained basmati rice and about 4 cups (1 litre) of water, or enough to cook the rice. Bring the pan to a boil over a medium heat and simmer for 10 minutes, or until the water has almost evaporated. Then cover the pot with a clean tea towel and a lid, and continue to steam over a low heat for 15 minutes, or until the rice is well cooked. Turn off the heat and let the palao rest for 10 minutes before serving in a large sharing plate.

THE MARKET WAS NOT REALLY A SAFE SPACE FOR WOMEN, let alone a pretty teenager who looked distinctly foreign. Local men came there looking for more than food. In some restaurants, waitresses did indeed offer their services. Hands moved in all directions, grabbing and caressing the waitresses, who had to make their way through the packed room, carrying hot plates of food. Taube was not a naive fool. She knew the risks she was running, but she needed the job. She also knew that she needed protection.

One habitué was a tall, blue-eyed young man from Minsk. Taube called him the Cossack, but his real name was Marik. After Minsk was occupied by Nazi Germany in 1941, he had fled south and settled – temporarily, like everyone else – in Leninabad. Day after day, he returned to the restaurant for his plate of rice or, occasionally, a bowl of shurpa soup made of odd vegetables and scraps of meat that the cook found in the market. Taube was fascinated by his refined appearance, his confident smile, his indifference to the catastrophe they were all living through. She also found that his company kept other men away. Gradually, from being a casual protector he became a friend, and perhaps something more.

Marik's presence reminded Taube of the everyday joys that she used to take for granted at home, in Riga. They could go dancing in the evening, or walk along the river in the afternoon. They could read the newspaper together, discussing the latest reports from the front. He could help her carry vegetables from the market to the kibitka and join the sisters for dinner. The promise of love and comfort must have been enticing after almost a year of hardship. The charming, broad-shouldered Marik offered her a future of love and stability. It was a tempting vision.

Good news came from the Russian front in 1943, as the Germans were defeated in the Battle of Stalingrad. The Russian offensive blocked any possibility that the Axis powers would arrive in Central Asia.[7] Despite the victory in the north, food remained scarce, and medicine for common diseases like dysentery and typhoid was almost impossible to find, even at the hospital where

Scheina worked. In the summer of 1943, Marik decided to return home to Minsk and join the Soviet resistance against the Nazi occupation. As his departure approached, he became restless and impatient. Why stay in Leninabad? he asked Taube, suggesting that as soon as the war was over she should join him up north, get married and meet his family. When he embarked on the train, he left behind him a trail of promises.

Without Marik's pleasingly distracting presence, the daily hardship felt more burdensome than usual. On her daily walk to the restaurant, Taube dropped into the Red Cross offices, hoping to find mail addressed to her. Usually she was up for a disappointment, but one day, she was surprised to find a letter. Rather than news from Marik, it was finally a note from her brother, Selik. He and the rest of the family were in Kurgan-Tyube (Qurgonteppa, or today's Bukhtar), a Tajik city some 400km south of Leninabad, towards the Afghan border. Selik wrote to Taube about the events of the past months, about hunger, disease and suffering. She read about the devastating loss of her younger sister, Sima, and her namesake baby niece, Taube-Mere. Small and frail, they hadn't survived the long months of malnutrition and illness. They shared a horrible fate with thousands of refugees who sought salvation in Central Asia but lost their lives there.

Taube and Scheina were impatient to see their family again and used their savings to pay for the trip to Kurgan-Tyube. The mountain passage across the dramatic Zarafshan range was long, slow and potentially dangerous for two foreign women and a baby. Even today, the railway is very slow and unrecommended. The road trip took Taube and Scheina the whole night, passing through Stalinabad, today's Dushanbe, and south through the valley until they reached the riverside city. Selik was waiting for them, and led them to the small house that the family had rented. It looked more modern than Taube's kibitka, but was just as sparsely furnished. All that mattered was that the family was reunited at last.

At the Adirim house, Taube also met a Polish man who rented one of the two bedrooms. Isaac Rosenboim was originally from Trzebinia, a small town in Polish Galicia not far from Oświęcim (later known as Auschwitz), where he had studied at one of the yeshivas, or religious schools.[8] He had trained in industrial knitting in nearby Kraków, with an eye to expanding the family's leather goods factory, but never had a chance actually to work in his profession.

Immediately after the German occupation of Trzebinia in September 1939, the Nazi authorities started confiscating Jewish factories and sending men to forced labour camps. In fear of Nazi persecution, Isaac's father, Solomon, encouraged him to leave town. The twenty-five-year-old Isaac would have been unable to withstand hard labour: he had been injured while working as a woodsman, leaving him with a limp. Unlike his married brothers and sisters, he had no family of his own, no particular ties to keep him in Trzebinia. In early 1940, he left his hometown and extended family for an unknown destination. Like the Adirims, he wandered about Central Asia in search of a sanctuary, ending up, somehow, in Kurgan-Tyube. With his shy smile and endless repertoire of Yiddish jokes, he soon became more than a tenant in the Adirim home.

In the autumn of 1943, Taube was nineteen years old, an independent young woman who worked for a living, chain-smoked Russian cigarettes, cooked for her family and went dancing with friends, despite her precarious existence as a refugee in an unfamiliar country. But more than anything else, her mother was worried by Taube's stories of this unknown Minski Cossack with romantic pretentions. Esther decided that the family should all return to Leninabad together, to keep an eye on Taube and perhaps prevent the inconvenient match. Selik invited the young Pole to join them.

In Leninabad, Esther sought to re-establish her authority as the head of the family. First of all, she took over cooking again. Taube continued to bring the groceries home, with the help of her sisters, but Esther decided what to cook and how. Cooking together was also an opportunity to talk with her daughter about her future prospects. Yet when her mother insisted she should go out with Isaac, Taube was not impressed. He didn't have Marik's looks or charm, and his stiff leg meant he could not dance. He led a religious life, observing the laws of kashrut, in an almost offensive contrast with her secular and socialist upbringing. She felt that they had nothing in common and was still set on travelling to Minsk to reunite with Marik as soon as the war was over. Years later, she used to tell her grandchildren that what made her change her mind was not her mother's insistence, but an invitation to the cinema. When Isaac bought her tickets to the movies, a rare treat that only became a possibility towards the end of the war, she conceded to go out with him. After three weeks of dating, they fell in love. Marik continued to send Taube letters, inviting her to Minsk, but she never answered.

Isaac and Taube's blooming romance was shadowed by growing family concerns for Selik. Having deserted the army in Gorky, he risked a court martial if he was caught by one of the officers who patrolled the bazaar every day. Afraid for his life, he returned to Kurgan-Tyube, and his son, Hatzkel, came up with a solution: since Isaac had two travel documents – a Polish passport and a disability card that guaranteed military exemption – the two men could share his identity. Selik would keep the passport, and Isaac would use the disability card. It was a feasible solution, as long as they did not live in the same small town, where the fraud could be easily discovered.

In the autumn of 1944, after celebrating the Jewish New Year with the reunited family, Taube and Isaac decided to leave Leninabad and return south, to Kurgan-Tyube, allowing Selik, his wife and son to live in Leninabad with the rest of the family. They were married on a Monday afternoon in a small, religious cere-mony officiated by a rabbi who was, like them, a refugee. After the wedding, they set off to start a new life together. When Taube told Isaac that she missed her siblings, and the joyous laughter of her young nephews and nieces, he encouraged her that they should start a family of their own. In the spring of 1945, when the news of the end of the war reached the people of Kurgan-Tyube, Taube was expecting her first child.

The end of the war meant that the millions of people who had left their places of origin during the conflict – willingly or not – were now moving around Europe in search of a new home.[9] It was one of the largest migration waves in modern history. Millions of refugees, evacuees, survivors, displaced persons and stateless people were crowding the roads and the trains, or hitching a ride on American military cars. While some sought to return home, to the place they had left, others were hoping to migrate elsewhere and start afresh. The sheer scale of mobility in the continent made it a political problem, and by the end of 1945, the victorious powers agreed that the United Nations Relief and Rehabilitation Agencies (UNRRA) should arrange the mass repatriation of all the displaced persons – a new term invented for this purpose.[10]

Soon after the end of the war, the authorities in the Soviet Union were keen that all evacuees and refugees within its territories should return to their countries of origin. After years of displacement, many longed for a normal life in their 'homeland', but not all refugees found the prospect of living under a communist regime appealing.[11] Esther had long wished to return to the safety of her flat in Stabu Iela. Harry's wife Sara also decided to return to Riga to wait for her husband's return from the war, not yet knowing that he had been killed in battle two years earlier.[12]

Taube did not see her family's future in Poland or Latvia, or anywhere under Soviet rule. Since she had married a Pole, she was expected to give up her Latvian citizenship, become Polish and return to Trzebinia with Isaac. At Isaac's request, she agreed to travel with him to his hometown to find out what had happened to his relatives and the property he had left behind. She had, however, no intention of settling down in Poland; from there she planned to reach a displaced persons' camp and emigrate to Palestine, the United States or some other destination.

In the spring of 1946, Taube, Isaac and their baby boy boarded a northbound cattle wagon that would take them from Central Asia to Polish Galicia. After a long– over 4,600km – and uncomfortable journey, they at last reached Trzebinia, or Tchibin in Yiddish. Isaac's family had lived in this town since the eighteenth century: they were there when Trzebinia was a mining settlement in the Lesser Poland province of the Polish crown, and when, in 1772, it was annexed by Austria as part of Galicia.[13] They benefited from the village's industrialization when it was part of the free city of Kraków (1815–46), and the family became famous across Galicia for their fur and leather manufacture. Within the large Rosenboim family of Trzebinia, Isaac's grandfather, Berish, seemed to have done particularly well: in a notary archive I've discovered that he owned a high-end fur shop in central Kraków and was able to buy out his siblings' shares in their father's house in Trzebinia.[14] In one of the few surviving photos of pre-war Trzebinia, the Rosenboim family house appears spacious and well positioned, just around the corner from Rynek Square, the town's picturesque central market. In this whitewashed, two-storey house with red-tile roof, Isaac grew up.

When Taube and Isaac returned to Trzebinia in the summer of 1946, they were unable to find a single member of Isaac's large family. No sign was left of the dozens and dozens of Rosenboims who had lived there for centuries. Isaac took Taube to see his father's house only to discover that other people lived there. Having perhaps recognized Isaac as the previous owner's son, who could challenge their appropriation of the house, they refused to help and aggressively chased the young couple away. Isaac was unable to discover how the family lost ownership of the house and the leather factory. Perhaps the Soviet governors requisitioned the property and gave it to their supporters, or maybe the neighbours got hold of the property after the Nazis deported its owners to extermination camps.

The disappearance of the Rosenboims seemed surreal. Isaac spent a few days trying to investigate what had happened to his parents, to his sister Bluma and her husband Hezkel Mendleberg, to his brothers Hirsch and Moses. But he could find no information at all. The local people refused to talk to him, but it was evident that all of his relatives, dozens of uncles, aunts, cousins and nephews, were dead. Years later he would find out that a couple of nephews had lived through the war and survived concentration camps and then emigrated to the United States and Germany.

The hostility of the people of Trzebinia towards those who fled and managed to return convinced Taube and Isaac to build their home elsewhere. Yet, like hundreds of thousands of refugees in Europe, they discovered that the communist authorities sought to prevent them from leaving, and few other countries were willing to accept them. Their main hope was to reach the displaced persons' (DP) camps set up by the Allied powers in Germany and Austria.

The DP camps were where migration decisions were made – or imposed on refugees in many cases – while 'normalizing' and 'rehabilitating' lives until they would be settled in a permanent home.[15] Being in a DP camp meant that sooner or later, you would leave. The humanitarian workers in the DP camps were in charge not only of the residents' well-being, but also of planning their future by helping them apply for immigration permits. As a Polish Jew, Isaac could seek international protection in a DP camp, and his wife Taube could join him too. After six months in a large, disorganized camp in Austria, they were transferred to one of the smaller American-run camps, Bad Reichenhall.[16]

Located in a charming resort town near Salzburg, Bad Reichenhall accommodated more than six thousand Jewish DPs. When Taube, Isaac and their young son arrived there, the atrocities perpetrated in the concentration camps had become better known, prompting the Americans to treat the survivors with more generosity and kindness than before. The young family settled into a surprisingly comfortable life, where uncertainty was mitigated by a daily routine of comparative plenty and pleasure. They lacked nothing: they bathed in the local river, drank cold beer at the café and read Yiddish newspapers. They made friends with other couples, and their young children played together. They were later joined by Selik, his wife and son, who also arrived in

Bad Reichenhall and waited there for a permit to emigrate to the United States. They were all slowly returning to normal life.

But not everything in the camp was positive. To the residents' dismay, cooking and eating as individual families was either impossible or forbidden. The war was over, but though Europe had been liberated, these people were not free and were denied both the right and the opportunity to cook their favourite foods in their own kitchens. In the archives of UNRRA, I read about a discussion among the humanitarian workers, whether the refugees should be allowed to cook and eat in their own kitchen, or whether they would have to line up for their food – once again – in a communal facility.[17] The administrators were concerned about managing individual rations and controlling the hygiene conditions of privately cooked food. The result, however, was that once more the people who lived in the camp felt removed from what they considered to be the basic tenets of normal life: cooking one's favourite food in one's private home.

The camp was a limbo between old and new lives, and its residents inevitably passed their time imagining the future. The world that Taube and Isaac had known – whether in Riga or in Trzebinia – had changed beyond recognition. They were citizens of nations that no longer existed as independent states. Both Taube and Isaac had come of age in European republics that emerged from the ashes of the Russian Empire: Latvia and Poland had tried to become cosmopolitan modern democracies. In the interwar years, they built stable economies, developed thriving cultural lives and carved out a protected space for their cultural and religious minorities. In both cases, these attempts were short-lived and ended first in national authoritarianism and, later, occupation by the Soviet Union.

Taube wanted to settle down, to live in a place she could call her own. Where might such a place be? It was a hard decision to make. From the perspective of the individual residents of DP camps, choosing their immigration destination might have appeared a personal decision. Instead, their prospects were being negotiated over their heads by newly founded international organizations, the Allied powers and humanitarian associations that tried to help 'resettle' millions of European refugees.[18] The victorious nations that managed the DP camps also wanted to control the movement of migrants, trying to persuade DPs to repatriate, or challenging their claims that they were, in fact, refugees and not economic migrants seeking to benefit from the postwar upheaval. Each case was examined individually, carefully, by the migration officers of the destination countries, who assessed the background and motivations of the claimants. Taube and Isaac were just two out of hundreds of thousands of Jewish and non-Jewish refugees who needed to find a new home.

The DPs were offered various possible destinations. Some moved to Australia, to the United States, or opted to resettle in West Germany. Isaac, uprooted from the small town where his ancestors had lived for more than two centuries, was tempted by the promise of wealth and opportunities in the United States. Taube was less convinced by the American dream, but the news she received from her family in Latvia was not encouraging either. When the Adirims finally arrived back in Riga, they discovered that in their absence, another family was living in their flat in Stabu Iela. The Soviet authorities forced the two families to share the flat: one room each, and a kitchen in common.

Taube's thoughts went back to her father, who had engaged in debates about Zionism with his friends from the newspaper, or to the joyful days at Hashomer Hatzair, the Zionist socialist youth movement, when the guide Shmulik taught her Hebrew with the prospect of moving to Palestine one day, to live a life of social solidarity and equality. The idea of moving to Palestine seemed, somehow, always present as a fantasy vision in the background of her life. She had no idea about the reality of life there, and knew little about the history and culture of the Middle East. But she longed for the security that a community of equals could provide, and the dream offered by Zionism could mean just that. Selik was lucky enough to get immigration permits to the United States, but after having second thoughts, he decided to wait for permits to move to Palestine, like Taube.

Yet, the British government, which managed migration to mandatory Palestine, gave migration permits sparingly, believing that Jewish migrants were potential troublemakers who would only aggravate local political tensions. In the YIVO archives, I found photos of the protest rallies that the Jewish residents of Bad Reichenhall organized against the British migration policy to Palestine. Thousands of men, women and children marched, carrying posters in Yiddish asking to release 'our refugees'.[19] Taube and Isaac's desire for stability would have to wait. How long? No one could tell.

*Chapter 11*

# TOVA ROSENBOIM IN SOUTHERN TEL AVIV, 1950s

ISAAC ROSENBOIM WAS AFRAID OF HEIGHTS. IT WAS NOT usually a problem, but it meant that, in 1949, once his family finally obtained the desired permit to migrate to the newly founded state of Israel, he refused to fly from Salzburg to Tel Aviv. Instead, he, Taube and their son travelled by train to Naples, then by ship and a few days of rough sailing across the Mediterranean to Haifa.

On disembarking, they were immediately sent to a camp in Haderah, about 50km further south. It was one of twenty tent-cities that accommodated the more than ninety thousand immigrants who arrived in Israel that year.[1] The new arrivals were not called 'immigrants' but *olim*, or those who did 'Aliyah', which means ascent, both geographically and spiritually. It is a term only used to describe Jewish people who emigrated from the Diaspora to the land of Israel. From its inception, Israel's legal system was designed to encourage Aliyah, and to discourage non-Jewish migrants.

After more than a decade of displacement and strife, it did not seem to Taube and Isaac, coming to a country thousands of miles away from home, with no money or family, that they had special advantages. But in practice, they were able to settle in a country that denied many others the same right and forced most of its original Arab residents to become refugees. The new state vouched for their needs, provided temporary support, healthcare, food and housing. They did not notice at the time that the social policies which put that support in place were often prejudiced and discriminatory.[2]

The immigration officer allocated them a tent and gave them official citizenship documents, taking away their foreign passports. He gave Isaac an Israeli certificate of military exemption for disability and decided that Taube needed a new name, a Hebrew one. He suggested translating her name to Yona, which – like Taube – means dove. But, as resistant to authority as ever, she choose 'Tova'. It sounded more familiar to her and also had an inspired meaning: 'good'.

Their first winter in the tent-city was cold and wet. The roof leaked water onto the soggy beds, which Tova made with pedantic precision. Thousands of migrants walked up and down the muddy alleys between the tents, wondering what to do with themselves in this enforced state of idleness. Many lined up in front of the administrative office hoping for news about a permanent home, a new job or information about lost relatives. But national resources were scarce, unemployment was rocketing and the new arrivals were expected to stay put, be patient and wait.

Food was served free of charge in the central kitchen. It was here that Tova and Isaac first tasted some local staples: semolina porridge with cinnamon and a fermented milk drink called leben for breakfast, a salad of tomatoes, cucumbers and green spring onions seasoned with oil and lemon juice, chicken stew or hardboiled eggs and marinated olives for lunch, sliced white bread and maybe a slice of cheese or a sardine for dinner. But all too often, there was not enough to feed the growing number of residents, who were not allowed to work for a living nor prepare their own meals.[3] It was a strange welcome to their new country, where they were finally supposed to feel truly at home.

## ISRAELI SALAD

Finely chop 2 tomatoes and 2 cucumbers. If desired, add thinly sliced spring onions, a finely chopped bell pepper or grated radish. Season well with finely chopped parsley, salt, fresh lemon juice and oil.

THE CAMP WAS A TEMPORARY SOLUTION, BUT NO ONE could tell when a permanent one would come. Now Tova was expecting their second child and she desperately wanted a place to call her own. Fed up with the promises of the immigration officers, every morning she encouraged Isaac to travel by bus to Tel Aviv to look for a job. Unlike Tova, he had not learned Hebrew in his youth. His stiff leg made him unsuitable for work in construction, the only industry that still needed hired hands. His professional training in industrial knitting seemed too specific for local manufacturing needs and in any case, all jobs were managed by a socialist syndicate that he was politically opposed to. He was one of thousands of unemployed immigrants who filled the streets of Tel Aviv. Without contacts, useful skills or even a common language, he was left wandering about in the streets of the White City, uncertain of his next steps.

In spring 1950, Tel Aviv was still drunk on independence. The beach promenade swarmed with families enjoying walks in the sea breeze. There were building sites everywhere, as social housing inspired by Bauhaus architecture went up to accommodate the new immigrants. Downtown, the national theatre put on a production of *Hamlet* in Hebrew, and the national opera house staged Puccini's *Tosca*. On Dizengoff Street, the busy cafés were full of elegantly dressed couples, who danced to the tunes of the local orchestra until the early hours of the morning.[4]

Isaac had little time or money to enjoy the pleasures that Tel Aviv had to offer. When he was not looking – vainly – for a job, he tried to find Tova's cousin Baruch, the son of her mother's sister, who had moved to Palestine in 1933. But how does one go about finding a person in an unfamiliar city without speaking the language or knowing a single person? He decided to start at the city's military headquarters, where a patient clerk agreed to help. They found that there was a Baruch Simanowitsch on file, but he had died in the War of Independence.

One rainy morning, with the prospect of another long day of wandering between factories and workshops ahead of him, Isaac saw a small bakery behind the Tel Aviv central bus station. The aroma of hot bread drew him in, and he saw the three bakers sliding loaves of white bread into the hot oven. They offered him a chair and a hot bun, and the conversation flew in Yiddish. He told them of his fruitless efforts to get a job and of the disappointing discovery that his only relative in the new country, his wife's cousin, had been killed in the war. The short, stooped baker asked for the cousin's name, and when Isaac responded, he shouted back: 'But we have a friend called Baruch Simanowitsch!' Could it be the lost cousin? Isaac left a note with his name and address with the bakers, who gave him a bagful of fresh bread. The next day, Baruch showed up at Tova's tent. More than a decade had passed since their last meeting, as teenagers on a lakeside summer holiday near Kovno. His entire Lithuanian family had perished in the war, and for years he had been certain that his Latvian relatives had suffered a similar destiny. Surprised and delighted at finding Tova again, he promised to help them.

In the winter of 2022, I returned to Hagdud Ha-Ivri Street in downtown Tel Aviv where Tova and Isaac settled in the house that Baruch rented for them. The house was no more than a wooden hut with a tin roof in the Neve Sha'anan neighbourhood, right behind the central bus station. For decades, the area was home to the city's poor and destitute. Eventually, it became a focal point for drug addicts and sex workers, and more recently African immigrants and refugees. Now, it seems to be a huge building site, as urban development has reached even this rundown part of town. The long-time degraded slums have been replaced with shiny residential projects for hip high-tech workers. But when Tova settled down there, back in 1950, Neve Sha'anan was a dirty, chaotic and unattractive neighbourhood of small huts and shacks, a world away from Riga's boulevards, ice rink and opera house.

Baruch tried to find Isaac a job, but eventually, after calling in some favours, he managed to get one for Tova instead. Every morning, she walked to a little wafer factory in Yesod Hamaala Street, just one block north of their new home, leaving Isaac at home with their two children. For one Israeli lira per day, she stood for long hours by the steaming wafer maker, pouring the runny batter into cast-iron moulds. As soon as they were cooked, she had to lift the crisp wafers quickly out of the mould before they burned or broke, and carefully place each wafer on the cooling rack. Her colleagues stacked them in layers, filled them with cocoa- or lemon-flavoured cream and cut them into long fingers. The wafers were wrapped in silver paper and sent to grocery stores around the country in large tins. The work was difficult and required nimbleness, dexterity and concentration, which, at the time, were considered particularly feminine skills. Unsurprisingly, almost all the workers in the factory were women.

Wafers were certainly not a novelty for Tova. She grew up not far from Riga's legendary chocolate factory Laima, which produced wafers, cookies and much more. But in Israel, wafers symbolized a new culinary sophistication. When the new state was founded, and welcomed hundreds of thousands of migrants, the government launched a regime of economic austerity and food rationing. The idea was not exclusively Israeli: the plan to restrict and control food consumption and production was lifted from Britain, which had implemented similar measures during the war.[5] Through food rationing, the Israeli government influenced the very intimate aspects of its citizens' lives.

The diet dictated by the rationing regime was simple. Every family received food stamps for corn, sugar, meat, eggs, flour, rice, cheese, onions and biscuits. Children were allowed additional portions of milk and semolina, but very few extras were provided. The stamps could be exchanged for products only at specific local suppliers, including grocery stores, vegetable shops, butchers' shops, fishmongers' and dairies. At the shops, women would queue for hours to get their allocated food before the supply ran out. While city-dwellers were forced to rely on the meagre offering in the local shops, those who lived in agricultural settlements and kibbutzim could supplement the official provisions with fruit, vegetables, dairy and meat products from their own farms and orchards.

This policy of restriction and control was supposed to help feed the migrants, save foreign currency and stabilize the local economy, but also, at least according to the official narrative, to shape Israeli national identity around values of justice and equality. Furthermore, it was a way to encourage some local populations – the Arab Palestinians and Bedouins – to leave, by denying them food rations. Among the Jewish society, often unaware of the greater restrictions imposed on the non-Jewish populations, the rationing policy was met with resistance, frustration and eventually the formation of a thriving black market of forbidden and desirable goods.[6] Soon, it became clear that food rationing provided only an illusion of equality and solidarity: those with means and connections ate well, despite official restrictions. With high demand for tasty food that could be sold under the counter, the wafers that Tova produced in the little workshop were a luxurious delight.

As more and more immigrants poured into the new state – not only from postwar Europe but also from Middle Eastern and Arab countries – the pressure for housing and employment intensified. As migrants were allocated housing by the state, sometimes in unappealing and remote settlements, food rations became a means to prevent them from leaving their allocated accommodation, as the stamps could only be used in shops in the person's official place of residence. This system undermined the values of equality that were, supposedly, at the heart of the rationing policy, creating discriminatory hierarchies among

Jewish residents in the newly founded state, and between them and the Arab populations.[7]

Even if Tova and Isaac lacked the ability to move about easily, they were luckier than most – and perhaps more stubborn. The immigration office tried to offer them a flat in Azor, a Jewish settlement built over the Palestinian Arab town of Yazur, whose inhabitants were forced to leave during the 1948 war. Tova refused, insisting they should be housed in Tel Aviv. Her persistence paid off. Six years after disembarking at Haifa, they were allocated a subsidized apartment on the second floor of a simple block in Yad Eliahu, a new working-class neighbourhood built on sandy dunes south-east of Tel Aviv.

No. 6 Ein Gev Street was nothing fancy: a bedroom with a built-in cupboard, a living room, a dining room with a balcony, and a kitchen. The functional furniture was bought cheaply at the subsidized state factory Lakol, which meant 'for everyone'. The balcony overlooked a communal garden filled with plum trees where all the children would play until dinner time. It was Tova and Isaac's first and only home.

Tova finally had a kitchen of her own, and a modern one too. It had a cooking stove, cupboards, Formica countertop, a small Formica table and chairs, and a small balcony looking over the courtyard. There was no fridge: initially, she had to make do with an ice box. Yet, she did enjoy the luxury of a free-standing gas stove and oven. At last, she no longer had to cook over a spitting fire or on a dangerous kerosene lamp, as she had during the war years. She was no longer forced to eat in communal kitchens or to settle for scraps gathered at markets and restaurants. She could stock her cupboard with food she liked. At Isaac's request, she kept the kitchen kosher, with separate sets of pots, plates and cutlery for dairy and non-dairy food. This compromise, however, did not dampen her enthusiasm for the kitchen: it became more than a place for making food. Cooking was a way for Tova to gain a new sense of control over her life.

Every Wednesday, Tova sent Isaac to the big market with a shopping trolley and a list of the ingredients she needed: carrots and onions, white cabbage and sweet apples, margarine (they could not afford butter), whey cheese and fresh eggs. If Isaac forgot something – which would have inevitably resulted in scolding – she would pop down the street to Meir's grocery store, which stocked pricier goods but also her favourite brand of cigarettes and provided her with the latest local gossip, too.

For Tova, the way forward was to establish a rigid routine for the entire family. After years of instability, order became her top priority, and food was no exception. Lunch was the main meal of the day and she planned it in advance. Tova tried to cook the same dishes she had eaten in her childhood in Riga. The starter was always piping hot: a golden chicken broth with thin noodles, or a thick soup of pearl barley groats. On Sunday she would make fried meatballs and fresh cabbage salad. On Monday, fried chicken and fried potatoes, and on Tuesday, they had meatballs in an onion sauce with potato purée. On Wednesdays, when she was busy with the week's laundry, she cooked a lighter meat-free option, often milky rice with cinnamon or a pan-fried noodle kugel. Thursdays were for beetroot borsht with cream or a cod fillet cooked in tomato sauce. Every meal was accompanied by a salad of sliced tomatoes and cucumbers, lightly seasoned with oil and salt. The same salad, along with sliced bread, herring, and peppers filled with cottage cheese, provided their cold weekday suppers.

## FRIED MEATBALLS

Mix 300g of minced beef with 2 finely grated onions, 1 egg, 2 tablespoons of matzo meal or crispy breadcrumbs, and season with salt and pepper. Wet your hands and form the mixture into small, flat patties. Heat some oil in a frying pan and fry the meatballs until both sides are browned and crisp. Put them to cool on a rack. (Instead of frying, you can also cook the meatballs in a simple tomato sauce.)

On Friday evening, after Isaac returned from the synagogue, Tova would serve an elaborate dinner that took days to prepare. The meal would start with pan-fried carp, served hot, or with chopped chicken liver, served cold. Both were accompanied by small pickled cucumbers that Tova made herself and kept in a jar of brine on the kitchen counter.

## CHOPPED CHICKEN LIVER

Hard boil 3 eggs, then cool them down in cold water and shell them. Heat some oil in a frying pan. Fry 500g of fresh chicken livers until they turn golden, then remove them from the pan and allow them to cool in a bowl. Using the same pan, fry 3 roughly chopped onions until they are soft. Mix the onions with the livers and the eggs and then use a meat grinder to mince the livers and onions, together with the eggs. Season with salt and pepper.

## PICKLED CUCUMBERS

Prepare a sterilized glass jar with a lid. Choose some small, fresh, crisp cucumbers, enough to fill your chosen jar. Wash them well and trim the ends. Place the cucumbers snugly vertically in the jar. Now make the brine, using 1 teaspoon (5g) of salt for each cup (250ml) of water, and pour it on top of the cucumbers until they are fully covered. For extra flavour, you can add slices of garlic, whole black pepper and fresh dill leaves to the jar, making sure that all the contents are covered by water before closing the lid tightly. Keep in a warm place, away from direct sunlight, for 4–7 days, or until their flavour mellows, then keep in the refrigerator.

On special occasions, Tova would replace these starters with the fancier gefilte fish, a cold carp patty in aspic. Making gefilte fish required advance planning: on Wednesday,

Isaac would bring a whole live carp home from the market, and it would swim in the bathtub for two days, until Tova knocked it dead and transformed it into the familiar cold patties. The fish was served cold, with bright purple horseradish chrain that would make everyone's eyes water, and some challah bread to absorb the gelatine sauce.

# CHRAIN

Boil 3–4 large beetroot (about 1kg) until they are tender. Drain them, keeping ½ cup of the cooking water. Cool the beetroot under running water, and then peel and grate them finely. Peel and grate a large horseradish (about 250g). Mix the beets and the horseradish together, adding 1 teaspoon of salt, 2–3 tablespoons of sugar, 2–3 teaspoons of vinegar and 3 tablespoons of the beetroot cooking water (or more if the mixture seems dry). Store the chrain in the fridge in an airtight glass container.

A CLEAR CHICKEN SOUP USUALLY FOLLOWED, WITH THIN noodles or shkedei marak – soup mandels, bright yellow Israeli-manufactured croutons – floating happily in the aromatic broth. On holidays, she would make delicate kreplach or mighty kneidlach dumplings. The main course would be the chicken thighs, fished out of the soup and fried in the pan until crisp, served with cold boiled potato salad and pickled cucumbers.

By this point, no one was hungry any more, yet they continued eating under Tova's solicitous and slightly menacing gaze. Next came a small cup of fruit compote: red plums in the summer and dried apricots and raisins in the winter. The dinner then came to a close with two unmissable cakes from the Latvian culinary tradition, a cheesecake and an apple pie. The base of the pie was a sweet flaky pastry, pressed into the square tin by skilled fingers. Thinly sliced apples, dusted with cinnamon and sugar, were then layered on top. Finally, a pastry covered the apples, like the iron grille of a medieval window. The cheesecake was made with the same pastry, filled with a mixture of plain whey cheese sweetened with sugar and a drop of vanillin essence, in lieu of expensive real vanilla pods.

## APPLE PIE

In a large bowl, mix 2 cups (240g) of plain flour, 3 tablespoons (40g) of sugar, 1 teaspoon (5g) of baking powder and a pinch of salt. Add 150g of cold butter cut into cubes, and mix well. Add 3 egg yolks and mix just until a dough is formed. If the dough is too dry, add up to 4 tablespoons (60ml) of cold water. Flatten the dough into a round disc and leave it to chill for 1 hour. Peel and slice 7 Golden Delicious or Granny Smith apples and place them in a large bowl. Toss 3 tablespoons (45g) of brown sugar and 1–2 tablespoons of cinnamon (according to taste) over the apples and mix well until all the slices are well covered. Leave the apples to rest at room temperature for 30 minutes. Preheat the oven to 170°C (gas mark 3). Line a 20–22cm pie tin with baking paper. Now the pastry has chilled, roll it into a 1cm-thick disc and place it in the tin so that it covers the base and the sides (keep the leftover dough to make a lattice decoration if desired). Prick the base of the pie with a fork. Pack the apples into the tin, and pour any liquid that remained in the bowl over the fruit. Roll out the remaining dough, cut it into strips and arrange them in a lattice pattern on top of the apples. Put the pie carefully in the oven and bake for 45 minutes or until it is golden brown.

Tova never expected her husband or children to work as hard in the kitchen as she did. She did not explicitly demand gratitude, but as she emerged from the kitchen carrying plates of food, a glorious matriarch, she was determined that her efforts to feed her family well and plentifully were recognized. In exchange for her efforts, her husband and children had to eat whatever she served without making a fuss. After having cooked and cleaned for the whole day, and watching her family finish up their meal, she enjoyed sitting in her living room with Isaac, who poured himself a small glass of cognac, a little luxury kept in the drinking cabinet.

On Saturday mornings, after his return from morning prayers and before lunch was served, Isaac would make his favourite egg and onion salad. It was a simple cold dish that, in his book, did not entail actual cooking and could therefore be prepared during the Sabbath. He would stand on the small terrace, place his wooden cutting board on the marble parapet and chop the onion into tiny pieces with a large cleaver, an inappropriately big knife but, he argued, the only one that obtained the desired results. As he leant over the cutting board, the chopped onions would make him tear. He would mix in the chopped hardboiled egg, season it with salt and black pepper, and serve it on a slice of brown bread, either as the first course for lunch, or as a mid-morning snack, along with a fresh salad and some low-fat white cheese.

## EGG AND ONION SALAD

Grate or finely chop a hardboiled egg. Finely chop a medium-sized white onion. Mix the egg and onion together well, season with salt and freshly ground black pepper and serve on toasted brown bread.

THESE NORTHERN EUROPEAN DISHES WERE SO BLATANTLY inadequate for the Mediterranean climate that they must have raised eyebrows in Tel Aviv. But for Tova and Isaac, it was the only home cooking they had known. In the small, hot kitchen in southern Tel Aviv, Tova sought to escape from the humid air of the seaside city to the cool freshness of Riga. Embracing the simple preparations of her childhood was an attempt to preserve a piece of a world long gone. In Tel Aviv there was no rich sour cream nor any luscious berries as there had been in Jurmala, but there were other new ingredients to explore: red and yellow peppers, courgettes, aubergines, oranges, cauliflower, white melons, watermelon, olive oil and lemon juice. Even then, it was only when chicken liver was too expensive that she would give up on chopped liver and replace it with an aubergine salad that seemed to have a similar colour and texture. She regarded aubergines with suspicion, never conceding them a real place on her plate.[8]

She made efforts to acquire new skills, too. In 1950s Israel one of the fundamental tests of culinary belonging was to learn how to bake with a 'wonder pot', a ring-shaped aluminium cake tin with a matching lid that was used to make cakes on top of a special metal ring placed on the stove. A local invention, if used properly, it meant that there was no need for an oven to produce a light, beautifully risen, airy cake. I would later learn the hard way that this was no easy task. It required skill and patience to ensure that the cake would rise properly and bake evenly without burning. Every week, Tova made a lemon-scented 'torte' or a cocoa and vanilla marble cake in her round wonder pot, and serve it with a glass of hot tea to the friends who came to visit and play a hand of rummy.

## LEMON TORTE

Preheat the oven to 170°C (gas mark 3). Separate 5 eggs. Whisk the egg whites and ½ cup (125g) of sugar until they form stiff peaks. Beat the egg yolks with the juice of 1 lemon and 1 teaspoon of vanilla extract. Gently fold the egg whites into the yolks. When it is all mixed, fold in 1 cup and 2 tablespoons (140g) of sifted plain flour and 1 teaspoon of baking powder. Pour the mixture into a well-greased 22cm cake tin (or a wonder pot) and bake in the oven for about 40 minutes, or until the cake is golden and a skewer inserted in the middle of the cake comes out clean. After 10 minutes remove the cake from the tin to cool.

Tova and Isaac were at home in Tel Aviv. They were surrounded by people who had come from so many different places, from Riga to Salonica and Aleppo, from Galicia to Bucharest and Sofia. Each of them, in their own way, was trying to navigate between their past and the future. They continued to speak Yiddish at home, with some neighbours, and even with Meir the grocer, who, like many others in Yad Eliahu neighbourhood at the time, spoke it more fluently than Hebrew. They never felt they did not belong.

Tova and Isaac had their flat but still had no stable source of income. Tova decided that if Isaac could not get a job, they could try to make money by starting their first business. Down the road from their old hut on Hagdud Ha-Ivri Street stood Tel Aviv's first power station. In the 1920s, it had provided electricity to light the city's main thoroughfares, Allenby Street and Rothschild Boulevard, and eventually also connected Jaffa to the electricity network. By the early 1950s, the square art-deco building was thirty years old, its technology too outdated to sustain the needs of the growing population. It was no longer the sole energy supplier to the city, but it still provided backup support for the national electrical company. By 1955, Tova had somehow managed to obtain the licence to run the station's cafeteria.

Tova offered a homely, inexpensive menu, in line with the austerity forced on her by rationing, which still prevailed, and the preferences of the workers, who were predominantly of Eastern European descent. She made sandwiches with Isaac's egg salad, chopped liver, aubergine salad, pickled herring and sour cream, or fresh white cheese and sliced tomatoes. She prepared large trays of cheesecake and apple cake, round lemon torte sliced into generous portions, her cocoa and vanilla marble cake and hot sweet tea. Isaac helped her, serving, cleaning, even preparing the food during the mid-morning rush and the afternoon breaks, when dozens of hungry workers arrived at the cafeteria all at once.

The intensity of the daily routine was rewarded with a reliable salary. But just as the couple had started settling down in their new business, the power station was shut down, its workers transferred to a new larger station in the northern quarter of the city. The administrative workers who remained had no need of a large cafeteria. Tova and Isaac decided to try their luck and open a place of their own in Ben Yehuda Street.

In Tel Aviv, street kiosks had become the preferred option for light meals or snacks that would be picked up on the way to work or to the beach. The original kiosks were relics of the Ottoman era, located in small round pavilions in the avenues and squares where people promenaded on Saturday afternoons, or took midweek after-dinner walks with friends. The kiosks became an emblem of the Zionist imaginary of Tel Aviv, as a city designed to encourage informal social life outdoors.[9] After the establishment of the state of Israel and as the economy stabilized, more and more people could afford to eat out – at least a slice of cake or a sandwich – and new food and drink kiosks opened in the main streets.

Tova and Isaac opened a sort of 'kiosk', which wasn't a freestanding pavilion but a small shop on Ben Yehuda Street, a wide and busy commercial road in the core of the city's central residential area that extended north of Allenby Street, parallel to the sea. In 1958, the city's first high-rise building went up there, and its first supermarket opened. Here, only steps away from the beach, their modest shop offered home-made sandwiches, fresh cakes, jam biscuits, tea and coffee as well as cold drinks in all flavours and colours, a range of wrapped wafers, like the ones Tova used to make, chewing gum and candies, apricot leather, chocolates and mints.

## JAM BISCUITS

In a large bowl, make the dough by mixing 1¼ cups (180g) of plain flour, 3 tablespoons (40g) of sugar, 1 teaspoon (5g) of baking powder and a pinch of salt. Add 100g of cold butter cut into cubes, and mix well. Add 1 egg and mix just until it comes together in a dough. If the dough is too dry, add up to 3 tablespoons of cold water. Flatten the dough into a round disc and leave it to chill for an hour. When the dough has chilled, preheat the oven to 180°C (gas mark 4), put the dough on a floured surface and roll it into a 3mm-thick sheet. Cut round biscuits out of the dough and then, using a small round cutter, cut holes out of the middle of half of the biscuits. Line a baking sheet with baking paper, arrange the biscuits on top and bake in the oven for 10 minutes. When the biscuits are golden, remove them from the oven and leave to cool. Then, place a teaspoon of jam on the biscuits that don't have a hole, and a biscuit with a hole on top of each one.

EARLY EVERY MORNING, ISAAC AND TOVA TOOK A BUS TO the kiosk, set their freshly made goods on the counter and waited for customers. Business was slow and they were forced to open longer hours to make ends meet. Tova resented the unwelcome attentions of the grubby men who stumbled into the shop after dark and she took to going home early, leaving Isaac in charge. Kind and soft-spoken, he was no businessman and frequently offered customers drinks 'on the house'. All too soon, the kiosk was losing money and Tova put it up for sale. She found Isaac a job at a textile factory – finally using some of his original training in the knitting industry – while she retired to the life of a housewife. She dedicated herself with infinite passion to the smallest, most mundane tasks: folding sheets into perfect squares, cleaning the house until the floors shone. Things had to be done well, or not at all.

By 1954, Tova had not seen her family for ten years. Selik and his family lived close by – they had also emigrated to Israel from Bad Reichenhall after the war. But the rest of the Adirim family stayed in Riga, and by the early 1950s it was evident that they would not be allowed to leave. Tova wrote dozens of letters in Yiddish to her family in Latvia, and in return received photographs of wedding celebrations and plump babies, as well as a picture of her mother and brothers standing next to her father's grave. She saw snaps of the new life that her mother and siblings built in Riga, but meeting them was impossible. Even a short trip out of the Soviet Union required special permits that took years to obtain. The new global conflict – the Cold War – threatened to keep her family apart indefinitely.

Tova would not give up easily. She dedicated hours to correspondence and filled in forms in round and orderly handwriting, requesting permission for her mother and sisters to visit her in Tel Aviv. For years, her requests were rejected or ignored. When she finally got permission to invite her sister Scheina to visit, there was a tacit understanding that her husband and daughters would suffer at the hands of the authorities if she did not return.

In 1957, Esther was, at last, allowed to travel to Israel. Tova was ecstatic to welcome her mother in the arrivals hall of Lod Airport. She settled her mother comfortably in the living room of the small family flat in Ein Gev Street, and they spent their days chatting, cooking and taking care of Tova's three young children, who finally met their grandmother. Although Esther was only in her early seventies, her body was frail, exhausted by displacement and tragedy. In the Mediterranean heat, she suffered from hypertension that weakened her heart. Despite Tova's efforts to sustain and cure her mother, Esther's health deteriorated, and shortly after her arrival in Tel Aviv, she died.

Tova continued to search for the relatives and friends she had lost to displacement and migration. In the early 1970s, on holiday in Kfar Blum, a kibbutz in northern Israel founded by Baltic immigrants, she accidentally met Abrasha. After his release from the Siberian gulag, he had married, left the Soviet Union and settled down in Israel. Their emotional encounter led to a renewed friendship, yet Tova felt that Abrasha was deeply transformed by his imprisonment. There was a new undertone of distrust between them, which her memories of affection and tenderness could not dissolve. Soon afterwards, the rest of the Adirim family were also allowed to emigrate to Israel. Tova was thrilled to have Leib, Scheina, Luba, their spouses and children by her side again. By then, however, they had endured three decades of Soviet rule. To Tova's three children, and maybe even to herself, they seemed irredeemably foreign.

# Chapter 12

# SHULAMIT EFRATI IN NORTHERN TEL AVIV, 1960s

AFTER THE SECOND WORLD WAR, THE ASHEROFF AND Mizrahi families both settled down in the working-class Shapira neighbourhood in southern Tel Aviv. Joya Mizrahi and her sons, Yitzhak and Shmuel, shared a small and humble shack, and Shulamit lived with her parents and younger brother in a larger semi-detached house surrounded by a small garden. Tova and Isaac Rosenboim's rented hut was also close by. They all arrived in Tel Aviv from near and far because they saw their future in the city and hoped that the opportunities it offered would help them live a good and comfortable life. None of them considered moving anywhere else, least of all emigrating abroad. Even if they had no clear vision of their future, they at least knew it would take place in Tel Aviv.

The aspiration to be local, to belong to the place where they lived and nowhere else, was what brought Shulamit and Yitzhak together. They first met in 1949, at an Israeli folk dance festival. The fixed choreography and the Hebrew songs in the background made folk dancing a popular pastime. Then, they continued to meet every week in Tel Aviv, walking along the main road from Shapira to the seaside, listening to classical music concerts or drinking fruit soda in the city's boulevards. Yitzhak seemed detached from the sort of family ties that prevented Shulamit from doing what she wanted. With no connections or property, he had a burning ambition to make it on his own, a desire that she respected and shared.

Yitzhak seemed to her to be deeply rooted in the young Israeli society. He was a soldier and a long-time member of the Zionist paramilitary organization Haganah and had fought for the defence of the Jewish Yeshuv. When Shulamit wanted to join the Haganah too, her father would not allow it, although his sister Penina used to be a member. During the 1948 war Hananya even bribed the registrar's clerk to forge Shulamit's year of birth in the official records, so that she appeared to be under eighteen and would not be recruited to the army (in response Shulamit cut off her thick black braids, and got a slap on her face). In a society forged by the experience of military service, Shulamit feared that she'd be left out. The only way to escape her father's domination seemed to be marriage, and Yitzhak's promises of rootedness and belonging ticked all the boxes.

Shulamit and Yitzhak were married in the last day of 1950. Her father was not enthusiastic about the match; he had hoped his daughter would marry the son of a wealthy Samarkandi merchant, and not a penniless orphan. The wedding gave Yitzhak the ultimate opportunity to put the past behind him, and he decided that his new family should have a new name. Sensing that Mizrahi was too Levantine a name to be acceptable to the increasingly dominant European Askhenazi majority, he opted for Efrati, after the descendants of the biblical tribe of Efraim.

A few years into their marriage, Yitzhak designed and built the family home in a northern quarter of Tel Aviv, a well-proportioned minimalist villa with a red-tiled roof, surrounded by a garden where he planted orange, lemon and tangerine trees. This part of town was so remote from the city centre that it was almost in the countryside, with fields of marigolds and sand dunes separating the houses and the small grocery store. Moving there was foolish, or courageous, depending on who you ask. It was certainly far from the bustling downtown area of Tel Aviv, but it offered Yitzhak and Shulamit a fresh start.

The house stood on a corner plot on Kehilat Odessa Street. It was raised above street level by a mound of fertile earth that had been specially brought in, held in place by a wall of pinkish-white Hebron stone. I remember climbing three steps to enter the house, but for decades there were only three unstable concrete blocks instead, until Yitzhak found the time to build proper steps. Next to the entrance there was a large window, enabling visitors to peek into the house and see who was around, or for the family to peer out at potential visitors. The main door gave on to the entrance hall: turn left to the living room and balcony, keep straight on for the kitchen, or turn right down the corridor to the bathroom and three bedrooms, two to the right and one to the left. Visitors often went directly to the kitchen and sat down by the dining table, while Shulamit cooked.

The kitchen itself was austere: whitewashed cupboards for pots and everyday plates, four large drawers for spices and utensils. A pale marble countertop and a large white ceramic sink under the window. A free-standing gas stove stood in the corner. Shulamit also owned a white Kenwood Chef mixer, which stood under a couple of simple shelves that held sugar, salt and coffee jars. The kitchen had a small balcony that was later enclosed and served as a pantry leading out to the vegetable garden. Yitzhak built it all himself, so the counter was a little too low, the cupboards did not close perfectly, and the drawers never ran smoothly.

The house was Yitzhak's great source of pride, a physical demonstration of his success in settling down. But it never seemed to be really finished, taking years to build, and it drained the family's budget. There was not much money for food. Once a week, Yitzhak would go to the Carmel market downtown and buy supplies for the week. In the long line of stalls and shops, stretching between Allenby Street and the beach, he bought only the most affordable seasonal fruit and vegetables.

In her new home Shulamit wanted to eat food that she considered local, and not Samarkandi food that seemed – to her or to others – foreign and strange. What food could be defined as 'local' in Tel Aviv in the late 1950s and early 1960s?[1] There was, perhaps, more than one answer to this question. Jerusalem-born Yitzhak considered local food to be the dishes that historically emerged from a variety of Sephardi, Jerusalem and Middle Eastern culinary traditions: hummus and tahini, cold charcoal-grilled aubergine mixed with tahini and garlic, stuffed peppers with meat and rice in tomato sauce, rice and lentil majadra covered with fried onions and, his favourite, sofrito, a potatoes, onion and beef stew seasoned with bay leaves and cinnamon and served with scented basmati rice. Shulamit abandoned the osh-sevo and goshgidja and cooked dishes that could not be easily associated with other places, nourishing food based on local agricultural produce.

In the early years of their marriage, Shulamit's cooking depended not only on her desire to belong, but also on the food rations that her family was allocated during Israel's austerity regime, which lasted until 1959. She tried to transform into plentiful meals whatever was available on food stamps – low-fat cheese, small portions of meat, onions, potatoes, a little rice and some lentils – and supplemented the limited supply with vegetables from her garden and eggs from her chickens. Even when, in the late 1950s, food was once again readily available, the family could not afford expensive ingredients. In the Lewinsky market downtown, Yitzhak could now buy basmati rice by the sack, but had to settle for the most affordable cuts of beef and chicken. Lamb and fresh fish were prohibitively expensive, well beyond the family's budget.

Shulamit devised a whole series of recipes to conceal the bland meat and render it delicious. She would vigorously beat the muscly beef steaks with a metal meat hammer to flatten them into thin slices, which she then dipped in egg, covered with breadcrumbs and fried until golden. She would cook cubes of beef in a sauce of tomatoes, potatoes, onions and sweet paprika. She fried crisp beef patties flavoured with chopped parsley, white pepper and plenty of onion. She also made a quick pasta bake with minced meat, fried onions and chopped herbs that would become appealingly golden and crisp on top. Some of these recipes disappeared from her repertoire once better meat became affordable, and she never served them to me. Yet sometimes she came up with long-lasting delicious recipes. Shulamit would prepare a flaky puff pastry beef roll, turning the home-made dough with butter or margarine, cooling and then rolling it open, filling it with a mixture of minced meat, parsley, onion and toasted pine nuts, and closing it into a long roll that she would brush with egg yolk and sprinkle with sesame seeds before baking. She also made fried meat and potato patties, which she would serve with lemony tahini sauce and a sliced tomato for a quick lunch. These dishes remained a sort of a constant reminder of the challenge that Yitzhak posed her, and of the additional work and compromises that economic hardship demanded.

## POTATO AND MEAT PATTIES

Boil 2 large potatoes until they are cooked but still firm, then peel them and allow them to cool. In a large bowl, use a fork to roughly mash the potatoes and mix in 250g of minced beef, 1 beaten egg, 1 tablespoon of olive oil and 1 tablespoon of crispy breadcrumbs or matzo meal. Finely chop a handful of parsley (about 20g), add it to the meat and season the mixture with salt and pepper. Using the palm of your hand, form the mixture into small patties and roll them in breadcrumbs. When they are all ready, heat some oil in a frying pan, and fry the patties over a low heat until they turn golden brown.

ONLY ON SPECIAL OCCASIONS, SHULAMIT'S CHILDHOOD dishes would infiltrate the family's menu. Bakhsh was a cheap yet flavoursome preparation that could also accommodate inexpensive cuts of meat without too many compromises, thanks to the abundance of coriander and sweet mint that dominated its flavours. In Tel Aviv, Shulamit simplified the traditional version, using chopped beef instead of mutton and liver, and with olive oil instead of lamb tail fat.

# SHULAMIT'S BAKHSH

In a large pot, place 400g of chopped or roughly minced beef and ¼ cup (60ml) of olive oil. Add enough water to cover it, bring to a boil and stir well. Finely chop 2 large bunches of coriander, and 3 tablespoons of dried mint leaves. Add the herbs to the meat mixture, season with salt and mix well. Add 2 cups (400g) of washed basmati rice and stir. Add more water to cover the rice and bring the pot to a boil. Cover the pot with a clean cloth and a lid, and allow to steam over a low heat for 20 minutes or until the rice is fluffy. Serve with fresh pomegranate seeds and a squeeze of lemon.

COOKING BAKHSH REQUIRED PLENTY OF CORIANDER. ON warm sunny afternoons, Shulamit's young daughters would wait in the street for the grey Peugeot van that sold fresh herbs. The car's driver was a man, but its passengers were all women, their heads covered in colourful scarfs in the style of Queen Elizabeth II. They travelled from the Arab villages in the north-east region to the vast fields that expanded by the Yarkon river, between Tel Aviv and Petah Tikva, where they would collect thick bunches of fresh coriander, parsley, mint and dill. They also grew artichokes, which they sold in bunches, like over-sized flowers tied by an elastic band. They would drive up the unpaved streets of the northern neighbourhoods, where Shulamit and Yitzhak lived, and launch their green bunches into the kids' hands, in exchange for a few coins. For Shulamit and her children, this must have been a rare occasion to meet the people who had lived in these territories for generations. Although Yitzhak and Shulamit grew up in the mixed society of mandate Palestine, by the early 1960s they had little interaction with – or interest in – the lives of the local Arab Palestinians.

In 1964, when his fourth child was born, Yitzhak decided to resign from his stable and desirable job in the electrical company and to open his own business. As an ex-soldier of the Haganah who had fought the war of 1948, he was entitled to get a shop in Jaffa. The original owners of the shop, which stood at the outskirts of the flea market, had fled the city during the Naqba. Like many other property-owners in Jaffa, they were considered 'absentees'. They were never allowed back, and their properties were repossessed by the state and redistributed to Jewish Israelis in an attempt to revive the once-bustling city that had lost many of its residents. Although Yitzhak recognized the injustice of taking over the possessions of refugees and refused to take legal ownership of the shop, he pragmatically agreed to rent it for a low fee.

By 1960, only two hundred families lived in Old Jaffa, although just fifteen years earlier the city as a whole had boasted a population of over ninety thousand. Now under the charge of the neighbouring Tel Aviv municipality, Jaffa was undergoing an intense transformation. According to the new municipal plans, Old Jaffa would become an artists' colony and a tourist attraction: local and international artists and craftsmen were invited to open their studios in abandoned shops, selling ceramics, jewellery, paintings and textiles. The Arab families who still inhabited the ancient buildings were forced by the municipal authorities to move to other parts of the city.[2]

At the outskirts of the market, Yitzhak opened a well-stocked hardware store. He sold all kinds of paints for walls, iron, wood and plaster. He had a German automatic key-copying machine that he considered the height of technological innovation. His shelves were full of drills, screws, brushes, hammers and saws of all kinds and sizes. He only stocked the best-quality goods, hoping to attract the builders, artisans, cobblers, craftsmen and carpenters who were working nearby.

The shop in Jaffa seemed to be in a different world from Yitzhak's home in northern Tel Aviv. It was surrounded by pitta bakeries and coffee shops with low stools where men sat sipping from small ceramic cups. There were also food shops run by new Jewish immigrants from the Balkans, like the famous Sami Bourekas, who sold delicious triangular Bulgarian filo pastry bourekas filled with salted cheese and long rolls filled with spinach, both served with deeply browned hardboiled eggs.

While Yitzhak would sometimes eat lunch out, at the bourekas shop or the hummus restaurant, Shulamit ate almost exclusively the food of her own making. The main exception were funerals and memorial services, when her extended family would gather to cook in honour of her dead mother, grandparents (Batya-Hannah died in 1948 and Zion died in 1959 at the age of ninety-six) and other relatives. For the descendants of Samarkandi and Bukharan migrants, remembrance of the dead was not a tragic gathering but a joyful culinary experience. This tradition seemed very alien to the mourning practices of the Ashkenazi Jews, who abhorred the connection between remembering the dead and eating good food; fasting seemed to them much more appropriate. For the Asheroff family, eating well could never be disrespectful.

I've heard many times of the magnificent feasts where the

family's older women served delicious fried fish with garlic and parsley sauce rolled in a pitta bread, baked bichak filled with spicy pumpkin, crispy noni-tokhi and fragrant palao with cubes of lamb meat, raisins and almonds. They were lengthy affairs, whole afternoons of eating and remembering together. Shulamit used to go alone – Yitzhak avoided death-related events that reminded him of losing his sister Luna in childhood – but sometimes she would take along her young daughter, and later my mother Ilana. These luxurious lunches, where unfamiliar relatives would offer her an endless succession of flavoursome and curious dishes that she had never encountered at home, became a cornerstone of the girl's culinary education.

At her home kitchen, Shulamit increasingly departed not only from Samarkandi recipes, but also from its minimalist way of cooking. She started adding in mixed spices that Yitzhak would bring from the market, which coloured her food in new shades of yellow, orange and red: sweet and spicy paprika, dried garlic, white pepper, turmeric, cinnamon, cloves, dried coriander, nigella and sesame seeds. She would also use mahlab to season her kaak, Yitzhak's favourite savoury cookies that the Ottomans brought to Jerusalem. Mahlab did not exist in Samarkandi cuisine, but there is, I think, a commonality of purpose among people who insist on spending so much time and energy in the lengthy process of extracting scents and aromas from hard, apparently impenetrable fruit pits. In Samarkandi cooking, apricot stones were typically split, then the kernels would be sun-dried and salted, to be eaten as a snack or ground into a powder used in traditional medicine. In addition to pleasing flavours, these kernels also contain poisonous cyanide compounds, but neither the Samarkandi nor the Ottomans seemed to mind.

# MAHLAB KAAK

Using a pestle and mortar, thinly grind 1 tablespoon (15g) of mahlab into a very fine powder (or you can use ground mahlab instead). In a small bowl, mix 2 teaspoons (10g) of fresh yeast with ⅔ cup (150ml) of warm water and 1 tablespoon (10g) of plain flour, and set aside for 20 minutes. Mix 2¼ cups (300g) of flour with 50g butter or margarine, the ground mahlab and 2 teaspoons of salt, and then add the water and yeast mixture. When a dough forms, add ¼ cup (60ml) of olive oil. If the dough is too sticky, add some more flour; if it is too dry, add some water. Cover the bowl with a clean tea towel and let the dough rise for an hour. Preheat the oven to 170°C (gas mark 3). Using your fingers, take a scoop of dough and shape it into a rope about 8–10cm long. Join both ends together to create a ring. Repeat with the remaining dough. Place the rings on a baking sheet lined with baking paper. Brush the rings with olive oil or beaten egg, and sprinkle some sesame seeds over them. Bake for about 25 minutes or until they look golden. Cool on a wire rack.

IN HER QUEST FOR 'LOCAL' FOOD THAT WAS DIFFERENT from her ancestral cuisine and therefore distinctly Israeli, Shulamit found inspiration in the recipes that women's magazines considered prestigious and desirable at the time. Often, these recipes were not local at all, in strict geographical terms. There were dishes borrowed from other migrant cuisines, brought along from faraway parts of the world, but somehow they were granted social acceptance and welcomed into the culinary consensus. Many were European dishes (German and Hungarian but not Polish) based on reasonably priced and accessible ingredients. One such recipe was the cake that Shulamit always made for birthday celebrations, the cake she would bring to the kindergarten or school for her daughters' parties.

In the 1960s, roulade was all the fashion: cakes, ice creams, meat dishes were all rolled up and sliced elegantly. The recipe columns in the newspapers were full of ideas for the home cook, and Shulamit's favourite was a simple sponge roulade, filled and covered with whipped cream or cooked chocolate cream, and, in season, decorated with fresh strawberries. Despite its Central European origins – and many global variants – it was accepted as a 'neutral' cake that was not tainted by any ethnic or diasporic affiliation.

# ROULADE

Preheat the oven to 170°C (gas mark 3). Line a flat rectangular baking tin (20x35cm) with well-greased baking paper. Make the sponge by separating 3 eggs and whisk the whites until they form soft peaks. Gradually add ½ cup (120g) of sugar and continue whisking until the eggs form stiff peaks. In a large bowl, beat the egg yolks with the juice of ½ a lemon and 1 teaspoon of vanilla extract. Using a spatula, carefully fold the egg whites into the egg yolk mixture, then fold in ¾ cup (100g) of sifted plain flour and 1 teaspoon (5g) of baking powder. Pour the mixture onto the tin and bake for about 10 minutes, or until the top is lightly golden. Spread a damp tea towel on a clean surface, and turn the baked sponge out onto the tea towel. Roll both the tea towel and the sponge together. Leave the roll to cool for 10 minutes, and then undo the roll, remove the tea towel and roll the sponge back into the roulade shape. While the cake cools, make the filling by separating 2 more eggs and whisking the egg whites with ¼ cup (60g) of sugar until they form stiff peaks. In a bain-marie, melt 100g good-quality dark chocolate and then vigorously mix the egg yolks into the melted chocolate. Let the chocolate cool a little, then gently fold the egg whites in. Cool the cream for at least 1 hour. When the cake is cool, open the roll and spread two-thirds of the cream on the inside. Roll it up again, and spread the rest of the cream over the roulade. As an alternative to chocolate cream, the roulade could be filled with 500ml of whipped cream, sweetened with 2 tablespoons (15g) of icing sugar. Decorate the roulade with strawberries or grated chocolate.

THE EFRATI FAMILY BLENDED IN WELL. TRUE, THEY aspired to relate more to the high-end villas across the main road than to the popular housing down the hill. But they felt at home. Yitzhak wore local clothing brands and got involved in labour politics. Shulamit took the children on summer holidays at a middle-class seaside pension in Naharia. Having shed any remnants of foreign culture and flavours, any hint of otherness, they felt that they no longer needed to prove their 'nativeness'. I am not sure if the choice to silence their histories was premeditated or not, but the distance between their past and present grew bigger with time. For Yitzhak, it eventually grew so big that no words could bridge it.

After the Six Days War in 1967, the wildflower fields that once surrounded the Efrati house were replaced with a quickly expanding neighbourhood of condominiums and villas. The Bedouins from the Negev desert whose sheep used to graze in the fields stopped coming. Yitzhak closed his hardware shop, which had gone bankrupt when he was away fighting the war, and Shulamit had to find a job as a pattern-maker in a local clothing factory. She still had to cook, but now had even less time and attention for it.

Only thirty years later, when Shulamit retired from work, did she return to her family's recipes. Liberated from the need to satisfy her husband's palate, to please her children or to adapt to the nationalistic social culinary norms of the young state, she started cooking the food that she used to eat at her parents' table. When I was in her kitchen, she prepared soup with hot fried meat dumplings that steamed with the first bite, something that she had rarely made for me before.

# FRIED MEAT DUMPLINGS

**(to serve with soup, recipe on page 43)**

Mix ½ cup (60g) of plain flour, 20g of fresh yeast and 1 tablespoon of sugar with 1 cup (250ml) of tepid water in a bowl and leave it to rise for 20 minutes. While you are waiting, fry 1 finely chopped onion in 1 tablespoon of olive oil, and then remove from the heat. Finely chop a generous bunch of parsley or coriander (or a mixture of both), and mix it with the fried onion and 300g of minced beef. Season the filling with salt and pepper. In a large bowl, place 1½ cups (180g) of flour, and add the risen yeast mixture to make a dough. If the dough is sticky, add a little flour. Knead it well and leave to rise for 1 hour. When it has risen, roll the dough into a rectangle about 5mm thick. Using a round cookie cutter or a cup, gently mark a row of circles on half the dough. Place a spoonful of filling in the middle of each circle, and then fold the remainder of the dough over to cover it. Using the cutter or cup, cut out the round dumplings, making sure the edges are well sealed. Heat 1 litre of deep-frying oil in a large pot. When the oil is hot (but not smoky!) fry the dumplings until they are golden on both sides. Let them cool slightly on a rack and serve warm, with red soup.

IN HER RETIREMENT, SHULAMIT ALSO HAD TIME TO START rolling and stuffing vine leaves again, picking young leaves from her own vine in the early days of the spring. Sometimes she made a meatless sirkaniz, which pleased the vegan members of the family, and on more festive occasions she even made her childhood's baked rice balls stuffed with meat and parsley that reminded me of Italian arancini. She embraced the beauty of her Central Asian culinary traditions, customs that remained relatively unknown in Israel until very recently, when the children of those who migrated to Israel from Soviet Uzbekistan in the 1970s opened fashionable restaurants selling these dishes. She was surprised to discover the enthusiasm for a culture that was once ridiculed, and even agreed to give some recipes to newspaper articles and TV shows proudly documenting the variety of Jewish diasporic cuisines.

It's not a coincidence that Shulamit's rediscovery of the repressed recipes of her past, in the late 1990s and early 2000s, was contemporaneous with a growing social awareness of all the cultural loss resulting from the Israeli attempt to forge a national melting pot. Many, like Shulamit, gave up on their unique – and foreign – identities in favour of a supposedly homogeneous local cuisine. There was never, however, an agreement on what such national cuisine might be.

Later on, greater social recognition of the value of diverse foods and culinary cultures (especially non-European ones) made Shulamit more comfortable about her own past. She not only cooked Samarkandi food, but also joined the Bukharan choir and participated in the community's social gatherings. Her family's Samarkandi food seemed to her not only desirable and tasty, but superior to other culinary traditions in Israel, and even to the food that she actually ate in Samarkand on her visit there, in her late seventies. She was no longer hiding her history of migration. Her family's food finally became her token of pride.

*Epilogue*

Twenty years ago, my parents, Ilana and Shlomi, also decided to migrate: they moved from their native city of Tel Aviv to a country house in Umbria in central Italy. The house was a medieval ruin that had been abandoned for decades and would take years to rebuild. In the fields surrounding it local farmers grew wheat, sunflowers or fava beans, on annual rotations. The crops reached right up to the house's decrepit walls, so that no patch of land was lost. The first thing my mother did in our new home, even before the construction works were finished, was transform the exhausted, intensely cultivated fields into a garden, that would continue the natural diversity of the nearby Mediterranean forest. Holding the dark, rich soil in her hands, she felt a special connection to the place she would now call home.

The garden became an opportunity to discover and revive the land's history. We travelled to heritage nurseries and selected ancient and rare apple trees, apricots and peaches, different kinds of figs and plums, and sweet-smelling wild roses. My mother, prepared a patch of land filled with a deep red fertile soil for a seasonal kitchen garden. She built triangular frames to support the tomato plants, which would yield enough fruit in the summer to make preserves for the whole year. She tied up the sweet peas to bamboo trellises, in the local manner, but also planted shrubs of coriander that the neighbours regarded with a suspicious disdain (the scent of coriander reminded them of that of a local insect). The olive grove hosted three local varieties of olives, Leccino, Frantoio and Moraiolo, that were suited to the Umbrian terrain and produced sweeter, gentler oil than the olives of Israel and Palestine. Planting our own trees was a way of spreading our roots in a new soil.

There was a special pleasure in eating and drinking food that we made ourselves, from scratch. But the making of the wine in September and the oil in November were also occasions to celebrate with others, to join local feasts. In Petah Tikva, Hananya Asheroff made wine from the grapes he brought from Samarkand. After the harvest, his children would tread on the grapes, barefoot in special tin tubs, until the cloudy purple juice tinted their legs dark, while Hananya and his guests feasted on a meal that Zoulay had prepared, in honour of the year's produce. We didn't bring in vines from Samarkand, or from Tel Aviv. Instead, we planted three varieties of grapes typical of the local hills, and formed the unique blend called Rosso di Montefalco. Out of the three grapes, two were migrants: the robust Sangiovese descended from Tuscany, and the adaptable Merlot came from France, but has found a home in many terrains around the world. The third was a very local variety, Sagrantino, that produces blood-red wine that is typically used for religious ceremonies in Umbria.

These tiny Sagrantino grapes, with their deep purple colour, are the best ones for baking the sweet focaccia that accompanies the annual harvest celebrations. After a long day at the vineyard, we would sit at a table in the garden together with the neighbours, Maurizio, Rossella, Giuseppe and Sandro, and other friends who came to help. We would drink some of last year's vintage and eat a warm, juicy focaccia filled with the grapes we had just finished collecting. In this scene, which seemed as if it might have been taken from a cliche-filled Hollywood movie, we found again the passion for eating together at the table, sharing the joy of food made with our own hands, in a land that became, at least for a moment in history, our home.

In the past two decades, I've been among those on the move. I cherished the freedom that I've found living in new places, making friends in new languages, and tasting new food. Migration brought me closer to my ancestors, whose lives have long been defined by mobility and shaped by the challenges and opportunities that it imposed. I felt that displacement made me redefine my own identity in relation to a new place, and I wondered how this feeling of otherness – maybe even unsurmountable foreignness – affected my great-grandparents.[1] Yet, as much as I felt close to my ancestors, their stories made me appreciate the safety of my own displacement, and the comforts of my home.

The legacies of their travels have remained alive at our dining table, where surprising and delicious interactions between the foods of Samarkand, Riga, Jerusalem and Umbria emerge every evening, with the occasional additions of Piedmontese dishes from the repertoire of my partner, Umberto. The trauma and penury of displacement were not erased but transformed, with time, into a familiar mix of wonderful flavours and scents.

Migration remains a highly controversial issue in contemporary political debates, and the rights of people on the move are often contested. Migrants are only a small fraction of humanity, but they have had a significant impact on the modern world. There is no international agreement about who counts as a migrant. For example, according to the International Organization for Migration, in 2022 fewer than 4 per cent of humankind – over a quarter of a billion people – live in a country other than the one in which they were born. Yet in some places, the impact of migration is strongly felt, transforming local economies, enhancing cultural diversity and creating cross-border communities. The interconnected world could not have existed as we know it without the decisive influence of human mobility.

Closed borders and the 'hostile environment' policy have not deterred people from moving. Whether formally defined as migrants, refugees, stateless people, asylum seekers or simply 'foreigners', people are still treated with hostility and suspicion. They are forced to fight for their rights and even struggle for survival in defiance of international treaties that are supposed to protect them. As I write this book, the world has seen new waves of refugees who have left their homes in Ukraine or Afghanistan in search of safety elsewhere. The tragic sights of men, women and children drowning in the English Channel and in the Mediterranean have become frequent again, but so far have not led the European governments to change their increasingly restrictive immigration policies. Migrants are still viewed as a problem to be resolved, as politicians come up with new schemes for their integration, or more often, deportation. But even when migrants are granted legal status, there are many other ways to signal exclusion, of which the question 'where are you *really* from?' is a striking reminder.

This book is my response to that question. The fragmented history of my migrating ancestors has taken me across borders and seas to Samarkand, Riga and the eastern Mediterranean, and back to my own kitchen, where the flavours of their past are still alive. Like millions of other migrants, my ancestors' past is a story of creativity, resilience and diversity which defies simplistic definitions of identity and belonging. Collecting and retelling the stories and recipes of migrants can be a form of resistance to contemporary exclusionary policies, and a way to imagine a different future.

# Acknowledgements

THIS BOOK WAS SIMMERING ON A LOW HEAT FOR A LONG time, and if it became a reality it is thanks to all those who encouraged and helped me along the way. First and foremost, my grandparents, Shulamit, Yitzhak and Tova, made this book possible (I've never met my grandfather Isaac, but memories of his wit and gentleness live on in our family). I will always be grateful for the hours we spent together eating delicious food and telling incredible stories. Grandma Tova used to say that her life's story could fill a book, and I wish she could have read this one.

Special thanks to my indefatigable agent, Sophie Scard, for believing in this project from its very beginning and for the enthusiastic and insightful comments along the way. Thank you to my editor George Morley, whose sharp eye improved the book immensely. The brilliant team at Picador (especially Rosie Shackles, Nicholas Blake and Jessica Cuthbert-Smith) has been a delight to work with.

Writing this book I've benefitted from the knowledge and generosity of many experts and scholars. Thank you to Olga Boloshko and Jakub Czupryński, who helped with archival research in Latvia and Poland. Many thanks to Ibrāhīm Šafi'ī, Ofir Haim, Max Malkiel, Merav Cohen and Habib Borjian for helping with translations from Judaeo-Tajik. I'm grateful to Peter Gatrell, Arthur

Asseraf, Maayan Hilel, Michal Ben-Yaakov, Anat Kidron, Zoya Arshavsky, Suzanne Levi-Sanchez, Ozan Özavcı, Antony Heywood, Gadi Elgazi, Arie Dubnov, Dafna Hirsch, Yair Wallach, Lior Erez, Nir Shafir, Marco Buttino, and Betty Banks for their generous advice and expert suggestions (all mistakes are my own, of course).

In 2019, I founded the Migrants' Supper Club in London, and started experimenting in cooking the history of my family. Many thanks to the guests and supporters of this project, for their curiosity about the stories and recipes that ended up in this book. I am grateful to Claudia Roden, who came for dinner and encouraged me to write about my family's food.

Thanks to my colleagues at City, University of London – and especially to Amnon Aran – for giving me the time to complete this project, and to the Robert Schuman Centre at the European University Institute, that provided the best place to write it.

I'm grateful to Edna Mintz, for safekeeping and translating her grandfather Zion Asher's memoir, and for her recipe for Bichak. Many thanks to Taube's niece, Riva Kapilevich, for sharing her family memories with me. I'm grateful to my aunt, Sara Levy, who preserved – and improved – many of the Adirim family's recipes, and to Galia Levy-Yanay for fine-tuning the Gefilte Fish recipe. Many thanks to Icheskel, Shifra and Ariel Adiram for the photos of Bad Reichenhall. While researching the book, I was happy to reconnect with long-lost family members, who enriched my knowledge of our ancestors. I am grateful to the Mirzoeff family in London – Eddie, Judith, Peter, Dan, and Jo – for the story and photos of Penina. Thank you to the Khalfon-Chen family, who shared details of Clara and Yosef's life in Egypt.

I cannot thank enough my wonderful parents, Ilana and Shlomi, who initially ignited my curiosity about our family's past, then let me tell their stories in my own way. Thank you for introducing me, at a very young age, to the worlds of good food.

Thank you to Umberto for lovingly (and patiently) sharing the pleasures and struggles of writing this story. This book is dedicated to our children, Alma and Ron.

# *Notes*

## 1 THE ROAD TRIPS OF ZION ASHEROFF, 1875–1882


1  Menahem Eshel, *Galleria: Dmuiot shel rashei yahadut Bukhara* [Gallery: Images of the Leaders of Bukhara's Jewry] (1965), pp. 138–9.
2  On the Jewish Mahalla in Samarkand see Marco Buttino, *Samarcanda: Storie in una città dal 1945 a oggi* (Viella, 2015), chapter 4.
3  Jennifer Keating, *On Arid Ground: Political Ecologies of Empire in Russian Central Asia* (Oxford University Press, 2022), p. 11.
4  On the Russian occupation of Central Asia see, for example, Alexander Morrison, *The Russian Conquest of Central Asia: A Study in Imperial Expansion, 1814–1914* (Cambridge University Press, 2020); Adeeb Khalid, *Central Asia: A New History from the Imperial Conquests to the Present* (Princeton University Press, 2021), chapter 5; Shoshana Keller, *Russia and Central Asia: Coexistence, Conquest, Convergence* (University of Toronto Press, 2020), chapter 3.
5  For a historical survey of the Jewish community in Bukhara and Samarkand see Michael Zand, 'Bukharan Jews', in Hano Tolmas (ed.), *Bukharan Jews: History, Language, Literature, Culture* (World Bukharian Jewish Congress, 2006), pp. 7–56.
6  On the relations between the Jewish community of Bukhara and Samarkand and its religious leaders see Giora Fuzailoff, *Yahadut Bukhara: Gdolea veMinhagea* [The Jewry of Bukhara: Its Leadership and Traditions] (Israeli Ministry of Education, 2008).
7  For a visual and architectonic analysis of the mahalla of Tashkent see Emanuel Christ et al., *Mahalla: The Survey* (Humboldt Books, 2021).

8 On fish in Syr Darya see https://livingasia.online/water/eng_taj_water

9 The citizenship rights of the Jewish residents of Samarkand and Bukhara under Russian imperial rule were long debated and negotiated. See Semyon Gitlin, *The Jews of Central Asia in Historical Documents 1860–1940* (Yad Ben-Zvi Press, 2018), part 2.

10 On Russian railways in the late nineteenth century see Edward Ames, 'A Century of Russian Railroad Construction: 1873–1936', *American Slavic and East European Review* 6:3/4 (1947), pp. 57–74; Anthony Heywood, 'The Most Catastrophic Question: Railway Development and Military Strategy in Late Imperial Russia', in T. Otte and K. Neilson (eds), *Railways and International Politics: Paths of Empire, 1848–1945* (Routledge, 2006), pp. 45–67; on Russian railways in Central Asia see Keating, *On Arid Ground*, chapter 2.

11 Louis A. Fishman, *Jews and Palestinians in the Late Ottoman Era, 1908–1914* (Edinburgh University Press, 2020).

## 2 BATYA-HANNAH ASHEROFF IN JERUSALEM AND SAMARKAND, 1887–1914

1 On the Bukharan community in Jerusalem see Giora Fuzailoff, *From Bukhara to Jerusalem* (Yad Ben-Zvi Press, 1995).

2 *Sefer takanot: Hevrat Hovevei Zion le-binyan batim ba'ad anshei Bukhara, Samarkand ve Tashkent.. be Yerushala'im* [Book of Laws: The Hovevei Zion Association for House Building for the People of Bukhara, Samarkand and Tashkent .. in Jerusalem] (Zukerman Press, 1891).

3 Dror Wahrman, *Habukharim u-shehunatam be-Yerushalaym* [The Bukharan and their Neighbourhood in Jerusalem] (Yad Ben-Zvi Press, 1991).

4 Ibid.

5 Abraham Asheroff is briefly mentioned in a biographic sketch of his son by his third wife, Rachel Douek. See David Tidhar, 'Eliezer Asheri (Asheroff)', *Entsiklopedyah le-halutse ha-yishuv u-vonav* [Encyclopedia of the Founders and Builders of Israel], (1956), Vol. 7, p. 2801.

6 Abraham Ascher, *The Revolution of 1905* (Stanford University Press, 2004).

## 3 ZOULAY ASHEROFF IN SAMARKAND, 1908–1924

1  Memoir of Hananya Asheroff, private collection.
2  Khalid, *Central Asia*, pp. 114–23.
3  On the Soviet attempts to influence the cultural and social habits of the Jewish communities of Central Asia see Zeev Levin, *Reclaiming the Hungry Steppe: Soviet Administration and Jews of Uzbekistan, 1917–1939* (Yad Ben-Zvi Press, 2012), chapter 2.
4  On the ubiquity of stuffed vine leaves in Jewish cuisine see Claudia Roden, *The Book of Jewish Food: An Odyssey from Samarkand and Vilna to the Present Day* (Knopf, 1996), p. 238.
5  For detailed accounts of agriculture and migration in rural Tajikistan see Monica Whitelock, *Beyond the Oxus* (John Murray, 2003).
6  Levin, *Reclaiming the Hungry Steppe*, chapter 6.
7  On the economic and agricultural crisis in Uzbekistan see ibid, chapter 4.
8  Thomas J. Barfield, *Afghanistan: A Cultural and Political History* (Princeton University Press, 2022).

## 4 THE ASHEROFF WOMEN IN JERUSALEM, 1927–1934

1  On the history of migration in Tajikistan and Uzbekistan see Kamoludin Abdullaev, 'Emigration Within, Across, and Beyond Central Asia in the Early Soviet Period from a Perspective of Translocality', in Manja Stephan-Emmrich and Philipp Schröder (eds), *Mobilities, Boundaries, and Travelling Ideas: Rethinking Translocality Beyond Central Asia and the Caucasus* (Open Book Publishers, 2018), pp. 61–88.
2  For a social history of Jewish Jerusalem see Yehoshua Ben-Arieh, *New Jewish City of Jerusalem during the British Mandate Period: Neighbourhoods, Houses, People* (Yad Ben-Zvi Press, 2011).
3  Wahrman, *Habukharim u-shehunatam bo-Yerushalaym*.
4  Sarah Irving, '1927: Earthquakes, Unemployment, and the Infrastructure of Mandate Palestine', *Journal of Palestine Studies* 52:1 (2023): pp. 3–20.
5  For a general account on the 'invention' of the four quarters of

Jerusalem see Matthew Teller, *Nine Quarters of Jerusalem: A New Biography of the Old City* (Profile Books, 2022).

6  The conventional and often sympathetic historical account of the Haganah is Ben Zion Dinur, Shaul Avigur et al. (eds), *Sefer Toldot HaHaganah* [History of the Haganah], (Hasifria Hazionit, 1964), vols 1–2.

7  Roden, *The Book of Jewish Food*, p. 454.

8  Ibid., p. 456.

## 5 ZOULAY ASHEROFF IN PETAH TIKVA, 1934–1942

1  On the relationship between the agricultural settlement and Zionism in Ottoman Palestine see Liora R. Halperin, *The Oldest Guard: Forging the Zionist Settler Past* (Stanford University Press, 2021).

2  Petah Tikva Municipal Council, 23 May 1934, ref. 001.001.003-274, Oded Yarkoni Historical Archives of Petah Tikva. This record is part of the Israel Archive Network project (IAN) and has been made accessible thanks to the collaborative efforts of the Oded Yarkoni Historical Archives of Petah Tikva, the Ministry of Jerusalem and Heritage and the National Library of Israel.

3  Menashe Davidzon, 'The Jewish Citrus Industry in Israel during the 20th Century', *Horizons in Geography* 64/65 (2005), pp. 425–37.

4  Anat Helman, 'Orchards and Shops: Everyday Life in Petah Tikvah of the 1920s and 1930s', *Zion* 3 (2005), pp. 338–55.

5  The electoral lists and protocols are available at the Petah Tikva Municipal Archive, ref. 008.006-1.

6  Petition to the municipal council of Petah Tikva, 6 January 1930, ref. 001.001.003/538, Oded Yarkoni Historical Archives of Petah Tikva.

7  'The Jews of Bukhara', interview with Hanania Asherov by Moshe Mossek, 1968, ref. 54(2), Oral History Division of the Avraham Harman Institute of Contemporary Jewry, Hebrew University of Jerusalem.

8  Zion's son, and Hananya's younger brother, wrote an account of his migration from Samarkand to Palestine, describing some aspects of Jewish cultural life in Central Asia. Shlomo Haim Asherov,

*MeSamarkand ad Petah Tikva* [From Samarkand to Petah Tikva] (Brit Yotzei Bukhara, 1977).

9 Residents' memories of the Blue Bird Café can be found in the local archives. See Oral Interviews, Box 6, ref. 01.04.05, Oded Yarkoni Historical Archives of Petah Tikva.

10 Ref. 001.001.003-684-1, Oded Yarkoni Historical Archives of Petah Tikva.

11 The British politics of rationing and starvation in Palestine during the Second World War is described in Sherene Seikaly, *Men of Capital: Scarcity and Economy in Mandate Palestine* (Stanford University Press, 2015).

12 On the air raids on Tel Aviv in 1940–1941 see Nir Arielli, '"Haifa Is Still Burning": Italian, German and French Air Raids on Palestine during the Second World War', *Middle Eastern Studies* 46:3 (2010), pp. 331–47.

## 6 A MEDITERRANEAN INTERLUDE

1 For a survey of the social history of Tiberias in the Ottoman period see Mustafa Abbasi, *Tiberias and its Arab Residents during the British Mandate, 1918–1948* (Yad Ben-Zvi Press, 2021), chapter 1.

2 'David Ben Naim', Montefiore Census 1875, ID 7982, Montefiore Endowment (www.montefioreendowment.org.uk/censuses).

3 Murat Özyüksel, *The Hejaz Railway and the Ottoman Empire: Modernity, Industrialisation and Ottoman Decline* (Bloomsbury, 2014).

4 On the Jewish community in Haifa see Yair Safran, 'Haifa Al-Jadida: The Surrounding Walls and the City Quarters', *Middle Eastern Studies* 51:3 (2015), pp. 452–61.

5 Özyüksel, *The Hejaz Railway and the Ottoman Empire*.

6 Alex Carmel, *The History of Haifa under Turkish Rule* (Pardes, 2002).

7 Michael M. Laskier, 'Aspects of the Activities of the Alliance Israélite Universelle in the Jewish Communities of the Middle East and North Africa: 1860–1918', *Modern Judaism* 3:2 (1983), pp. 147–71.

8 Yosef Khalfon's emigration is mentioned in a biographic sketch of his father, an important local leader in Haifa. See David Tidhar, 'Rabi

Abraham Raphael Khalfon', *Entsiklopedyah le-halutse ha-yishuv u-vonav*, vol. 2, p. 845.

9  On the influence of the Young Turks Revolution on the Arab communities in the Ottoman Empire see Hasan Kayalı, *Arabs and Young Turks: Ottomanism, Arabism and Islamism in the Ottoman Empire, 1908–1918* (University of California Press, 1997).

10  For the cultural and social history of Alexandria as a cosmopolitan city see Robert Ilbert, *Alexandrie, 1830–1930: Histoire d'une Communauté Citadine* (Institut Français d'Archéologie Orientale, 1996).

11  Roden, *The Book of Jewish Food*, p. 400.

12  Vincent Lemire, *Jerusalem, 1900: The Holy City in the Age of Possibilities*, trans. Catherine Tihanyi and Lys Ann Weiss (Chicago University Press, 2017).

13  On 'Ottomanist' Jews see Fishman, *Jews and Palestinians*.

14  For an analysis of the decline of the Ottoman Empire see M. Şükrü Hanioğlu, *A Brief History of the Late Ottoman Empire* (Princeton University Press, 2008).

15  On the Ottoman economy before and during the war see Ş Pamuk, 'The Ottoman Economy in World War I', in S. Broadberry and M. Harrison (eds), *The Economics of World War I* (Cambridge University Press, 2005), pp. 112–36.

16  On the economic crisis in Palestine after the First World War see Abigail Jacobson, 'A City Living through Crisis: Jerusalem during World War I', *British Journal of Middle Eastern Studies* 36:1 (2009), pp. 73–92.

17  On the tensions between Ottoman and Zionist ideologies see Michelle U. Campos, 'Between "Beloved Ottomania" and "The Land of Israel": The Struggle over Ottomanism and Zionism among Palestine's Sephardi Jews, 1908–13', *International Journal of Middle East Studies* 37:4 (2005), pp. 461–83.

## 7 JOYA MIZRAHI IN JERUSALEM, 1932–1936

1  Eliezer David Yafe, *Yemin Moshe: Sipura shel sh'chuna be Yerushala'im* [Yemin Moshe: The Story of a Neighbourhood in Jerusalem] (Ariel, 1985).

2  Craig Larkin et al., *The Struggle for Jerusalem's Holy Places* (Taylor & Francis, 2013).

3  On the history of the windmill and its English makers see Saul Sapir, 'From Canterbury to Jerusalem: New Disclosures about the English Windmill in Jerusalem, *Cathedra: For the History of Eretz Israel and Its Yishuv* 81 (1996), pp. 35–60.

4  For a personal memoir of growing up in Yemin Moshe during the British Mandate see Yaakov Yehoshua, *Shechunut be Yerushala'im Hayeshana: Pirkei havai me yamim avaru* [Neighbourhoods in old Jerusalem: Local stories of old times] (Mass, 1971).

5  Yehoshua Ben-Arieh, *The Making of Eretz Israel in the Modern Era: A Historical-Geographical Study (1799–1949)* (De Gruyter, 2020), chapter 9.

6  On the Sephardi community of Jerusalem see Abigail Jacobson, *From Empire to Empire: Jerusalem Between Ottoman and British Rule* (Syracuse University Press, 2011).

7  On ethnic tensions in Israeli society see for example A. Khazzoom, 'The Great Chain of Orientalism: Jewish Identity, Stigma Management, and Ethnic Exclusion in Israel', *American Sociological Review* 68:4 (2003), pp. 481–510.

8  On the long shadows of the Arab Revolt see Ted Swedenburg, *Memories of Revolt: The 1936–1939 Rebellion and the Palestinian National Past* (University of Arkansas Press, 2003).

9  Shaul Bartal, 'The Peel Commission Report of 1937 and the Origins of the Partition Concept' *Jewish Political Studies Review* 28:1/2 (2017), pp. 51–70; Penny Sinanoglou, 'British Plans for the Partition of Palestine, 1929–1938', *Historical Journal* 52:1 (2009), 131–52.

10  There were various interpretations of the Arab revolt, including for example Ghassan Kanafani, *The 1936–39 Revolt in Palestine* (Committee for a Democratic Palestine, 1972); Matthew Hughes, 'The Banality of Brutality: British Armed Forces and the Repression of the Arab Revolt in Palestine, 1936–39', *English Historical Review* 124:507 (2009), pp. 313–54; Jacob Norris, 'Repression and Rebellion: Britain's Response to the Arab Revolt in Palestine of 1936–39', *Journal of Imperial and Commonwealth History* 36:1 (2008), pp. 25–45.

11  Yehezkel and Joya Mizrahi, residents in Ruhama neighbourhood of Jerusalem, appear on Voters List Knesset Israel 1935, line 39, Israel Genealogy Research Association Database number 16249. The original records are from Israel State Archives.

12  For a history of Rishon Lezion and its winemaking industry see Dan Gileadi, 'Rishon Lezion under the Tutelage of the Baron Rothschild (1882–1900)', *Cathedra* 9 (1978), pp. 127–52.

## 8 ESTHER ADIRIM IN RIGA, 1928–1941

1  House register of Riga, Lačplēša Street 112a, file 8009, Latvian National Archives.

2  1st All Russian census of Rēzekne (former Rezhitsa) for 1897, fond 2706, inventory 1, file 157, pp. 307–10; birth records of the Jewish community in Rēzekne for 1880, fond 5024, inventory 1, file 255, p. 77; birth records of the Jewish community in Rēzekne for 1882, file 127; birth records of the Jewish community in Rēzekne for 1885, inventory 2, file 613; Latvian National Archives.

3  For a history of the Jewish community of Latvia see Dov Levin, *Pinḳas Haḳehilot. Laṭviyah ṿe Esṭonyah: Entsiḳlopedyah Shel Hayishuvim HaYehudiyim Lemin Hiṿasdam ṿeʿad Leaḥar Shoʿat Milḥemet Haolam Hasheniyah* [The Notebook of Communities: Encyclopedia of Jewish Communities from their Foundation to after the Holocaust] (Yad ṿa-shem, 1988); Māra Caune and Jānis Graudonis, *Latvijas pilsētas enciklopēdija redkolēģija* [Encyclopaedia of Latvian Cities] (Preses nams, 1999).

4  Passport Issuance Book of Ludza for 1922–4, fond 1412, inventory 3, file 948, pp. 45, 46, 54, Latvian National Archives.

5  There are few histories of Latvia in English; see, for example, Mara Kalnins, *Latvia: A Short History* (Hurst, 2015).

6  Levin, *Pinḳas Haḳehilot.*

7  For a personal memoir of growing up in Riga before the Second World War see Max Michelson, *City of Life, City of Death: Memories of Riga* (University Press of Colorado, 2001), chapter 3; Josifs Šteimanis, *Ḷatvijas ebreju vēsture* [History of Latvian Jews] (Saule, 1995).

8 For a historical survey of the old city of Riga see Andris Caune, *Rīgas klusais centrs pirms 100 gadiem* [The Quiet Centre of Riga 100 Years Ago] (Latvijas vēstures institūta apgāds, 2015).

9 Latvian passport of Schapiro, widow Adirim Gena-Rivka, inventory 17, file 4068, Latvian National Archives.

10 On the burning of the synagogues of Riga see Andrew Ezergailis, *The Holocaust in Latvia, 1941–1944: The Missing Center* (Historical Institute of Latvia and US Holocaust Memorial Museum, 1996), pp. 220ff; Andrej Angrick and Peter Klein, *The 'Final Solution' in Riga: Exploitation and Annihilation, 1941–1944* (Berghahn Books, 2012).

11 On kitchens in Riga before the Second World War see J. Irbe, I. Keviesans, G. Strauta and A. Zeltins, *Virtuves Labiericibas* [Kitchen Equipment] (Lavtijas Lauksaimniecibas kamera, 1940).

12 On Riga's market see Oskars Balodis and Dace Janone, *Rīgas centrāltirgus – iedvesmas vieta* [Riga's Central Market – A Place of Inspiration] (Apgāds Mantojums, 2013).

13 Aleksandrs Čaks, *Selected Poems*, trans. Ruth Speirs (Liesma, 1979).

14 Contemporary Western commentators were critical of Ulmanis's coup. See for example, Ralph Thompson, 'Latvia Turns from Democracy', *Current History* 40:4 (1934), pp. 499–501.

15 Vilma Bertina, *Praktiskā virtuve* [Practical Kitchen] (Atauga Press, 1939); Marija Leiše, *Kā sarīkot viesības un ko celt galdā* [How to Organize Parties and Lay the Table] (Spīdola, 1936).

16 Latvian passports of Esther Adirim, fond 2996, inventory 1, file 3898; fond 3234, inventory 33, file 94629, Latvian National Archives.

17 For an analysis of Latvia in Russian and German war strategies see Valdis O. Lumans, *Latvia in World War II* (Fordham University Press, 2021).

18 On the experience of Latvian evacuees and deportees see Tomas Balkelis and Violeta Davoliūtė, *Narratives of Exile and Identity: Soviet Deportation Memoirs from the Baltic States* (Central European University Press, 2018), pp. 85–100.

19 House Registers of Riga and Environs, Stabu Street 46/48, apt. 85, Riga, 22 July 1941, fond 2942, inventory 1, file 12777, Latvian National Archives.

20 For a detailed account of the experience of Jewish refugees in Central Asia see Albert Kaganovitch, *Exodus and Its Aftermath: Jewish Refugees in the Wartime Soviet Interior* (University of Wisconsin Press, 2022).

## 9 TAUBE ADIRIM IN GORKY, 1941

1 Maxim Gorky, *My Childhood*, trans. Gertrude M. Foakes (Penguin, 1991).

2 Lennart Samuelson, *Tankograd: The Formation of a Soviet Company Town: Cheliabinsk, 1900s–1950s* (Palgrave, 2011).

## 10 THE ADIRIM FAMILY IN LENINABAD, 1942–1946

1 On the Soviet repression of the local 'bourgeoisie' see Khalid, *Central Asia*, chapter 11.

2 For a detailed account of the struggles of the evacuees see Rebecca Manley, *To the Tashkent Station: Evacuation and Survival in the Soviet Union at War* (Cornell University Press, 2009).

3 On evacuees' memories of hunger in Central Asia see also Mikhal Dekel, *Tehran Children: A Holocaust Refugee Odyssey* (W. W. Norton, 2019).

4 On Leninabad, or Khujand, see Kamoludin Abdullaev, 'Khujand', *Historical Dictionary of Tajikistan* (Rowman & Littlefield, 2018), p. 241.

5 On the history of Tajikistan see for example Paul Bergne, *Birth of Tajikistan: National Identity and the Origins of the Republic* (IB Tauris, 2007); Christian Bleuer, 'State-building, Migration and Economic Development on the Frontiers of Northern Afghanistan and Southern Tajikistan', *Journal of Eurasian Studies* 3:1 (2012), pp. 69–79.

6 Eliyana R. Adler, *Survival on the Margins: Polish Jewish Refugees in the Wartime Soviet Union* (Harvard University Press, 2020).

7 On the military history of the Soviet campaigns see, for example, D. Stone, 'Operations on the Eastern Front, 1941–1945', in J. Ferris and E. Mawdsley (eds), *The Cambridge History of the Second World War* (Cambridge University Press, 2015), pp. 331–57.

8 For a cultural history of the region of Galicia under the Austro-

Hungarian Empire see Martin Pollack, *Galizia: Viaggio nel cuore scomparso della Mittleuropa* (Keller, 2017).

9  On the experiences of refugees and displaced persons in wartime and postwar Europe see Peter Gatrell, *The Unsettling of Europe: The Great Migration, 1945 to the Present* (Penguin, 2019).

10  For a recent history of DP camps see David Nasaw, *The Last Million: Europe's Displaced Persons from World War to Cold War* (Penguin, 2020).

11  Seth Bernstein, *Return to the Motherland: Displaced Soviets in WWII and the Cold War* (Cornell University Press, 2023).

12  Evidence on Hirsch (Harry) Adirim's death in battle can be found on the OBD Memorial, an initiative of the Russian Ministry of Defence, which collects data and documents about Soviet military deaths during the Great Patriotic War, https://obd-memorial.ru/html/info.htm?id=1935051

13  The earliest evidence of the Rosenboim (spelled also Rosenbaum) family's presence in Trzebinia can be found in Trzebinia Land and Mortage records (1826–1876), Kraków National Archives/465/202-203

14  The deed for the Rosenbaum house in Trzebinia, bought by Isaac Rosenbaum's grandfather Beresh, can be found in Notary Romowicz in Chrzanów, ref. 930/LRep#26863, Kraków National Archives.

15  Nasaw, *The Last Million*, chapter 18.

16  Taube Rosenbaum, Postwar Card File (A–Z), 03010101 0S/68826116, Digital Archive, Arolsen Archives.

17  Evidence of the challenges of cooking and eating in the DP camps can be found in administrative correspondence, such as Deputy Chief, D. P. Operations to D. P. Field Representative, Milan and All Camp Directors, 12 March 1947, Displaced Persons Operations – Italy – Food Distribution in Camps, ref. S-1479-0000-0056, United Nations Relief and Rehabilitation Administration Archives.

18  The difficult return of Jewish refugees to Soviet Russia is described in Albert Kaganovitch, 'Stalin's Great Power Politics, the Return of Jewish Refugees to Poland, and Continued Migration to Palestine, 1944–1946', *Holocaust and Genocide Studies* 26:1 (2012), pp. 59–94.

19  The Bad Reichenhall's photo collection in the YIVO archive (Yidisher Visnshaftlekher Institut, or Yiddish Scientific Institute) includes

evidence of political rallies. Protests against British immigration policy to Palestine, RG 294.5, Folder 10, YIVO Displaced Persons Camps and Centers Photograph Collection, https://digipres.cjh.org/delivery/DeliveryManagerServlet?dps_pid=IE3152103

## 11 TOVA ROSENBOIM IN SOUTHERN TEL AVIV, 1950S

1   On life in migrant camps in the 1950s see Aharon Yaffe, 'The Gate of Aliya – The Camp and Its Services', *Horizons in Geography* 96 (2019), pp. 27–40.

2   On Palestinian refugees after 1948 see Anne Irfan, *Refuge and Resistance: Palestinians and the International Refugee System* (Columbia University Press, 2023).

3   Yaffe, 'The Gate of Aliya', p. 35.

4   On the social and cultural significance of Dizengoff Street see Maoz Azaryahu, *Tel Aviv: Mythography of a City* (Syracuse University Press, 2007), pp. 106–24.

5   On various wartime means to control and restrict food consumption see Rachel Duffett, Ina Zweiniger-Bargielowska and Alain Drouard (eds), *Food and War in Twentieth Century Europe* (Routledge, 2016).

6   For a general overview of food rationing policies in Israel see Orit Rozin, 'Food, Identity, and Nation-Building in Israel's Formative Years', *Israel Studies Forum* 21:1 (2006), pp. 52–80.

7   For a critical account of the rationing system in Jewish and non-Jewish communities see Gadi Algazi, 'Food, Hunger and Colonization in the Early 1950s', paper presented at the international workshop 'Is There an Israeli History without Palestinian History?', Van Leer Jerusalem Institute, 14–15 September 2022 (unpublished).

8   Ari Ariel, 'Mosaic or Melting Pot: The Transformation of Middle Eastern Jewish Foodways in Israel', in Hasia R. Diner and Simone Cinotto (eds), *Global Jewish Foodways* (University of Nebraska Press, 2018), pp. 91–114.

9   On popular leisure sites in Tel Aviv, such as Rothschild Boulevard, see Barbara Mann, 'Tel Aviv's Rothschild: When a Boulevard Becomes a Monument', *Jewish Social Studies* 7:2 (2001), pp. 1–38.

## 12 SHULAMIT EFRATI IN NORTHERN TEL AVIV, 1960S

1 On the history of food and nationalism in Israel see Yael Raviv, *Falafel Nation: Cuisine and the Making of National Identity in Israel* (University of Nebraska Press, 2015).
2 On the erasure of Arab culture in Tel Aviv-Jaffa see Sharon Rotbard, *White City, Black City: Architecture and War in Tel Aviv and Jaffa,* trans. Orit Gat (MIT Press, 2015).

## EPILOGUE

1 Richard Sennett, *The Foreigner: Two Essays on Exile* (Notting Hill Editions, 2011).